ABOUT THE AUTHOR

Steve Atherton is the founder of 56NOTOUT which continues to raise funds and awareness for the homeless. As a qualified running coach, He is also one of the founder members of a Run England running group *Zero to Hero* which encourages and motivates people to start running.

He works in the automotive industry and was born in Royal Leamington Spa. Steve now lives in Warwick with his wife Julie and Louis and Leo the cats.

He has two daughters, two step - daughters and three grandchildren.

He is 58 but will forever be Mr 56.

EST'D 1961

THE
56
NOT OUT
CHALLENGE

FULL OF VARIETY

56 NOT OUT

One Man - One Year —
56 Challenges

STEVE ATHERTON

Published 2019, in Great Britain,

Text Copyright © Steve Atherton 2019

All rights reserved. No part of this publication may be reproduced, stored
in a retrieval system, or transmitted in any form or by any means,
electronic, mechanical, photocopy, recording or otherwise, without prior
written permission of the copyright owner. Nor can it be circulated in any
form of binding or cover other than that in which it is published and
without similar condition including this condition being imposed on a
subsequent purchaser.

British Cataloguing Publication data:
A catalogue record of this book is available from
the British Library

This book is also available as an ebook.

I dedicate this book to my wife, Julie and my family.

Family is everything!

CONTENTS

FOREWORD

Welcome to the story of 56notout.

When Steve announced one morning that he was thinking of doing a year of challenges to mark his 56th birthday I must admit I didn't think too much about it. That's nice dear...

Fast forward to a year later and I was standing on stage with some of the other 56notout team accepting his special achievement award at the Pride of Warwickshire awards.

As I made my speech, I realised what a monumental achievement it was, it was an emotional moment.

The year flew by in a crazy blur, I don't think either of us realised the amount of work and planning it would take.

I didn't expect to be alongside Steve swimming the freezing Serpentine, dragging him onto rollercoasters, buying clothes to dress him as a drag queen and waving him off for pole dancing lessons!

We met some wonderful, interesting people who helped with the challenges and thank them all.

This year opened my eyes to the real issues of homelessness and our contribution is a drop in the ocean compared to the people who tirelessly work to give people a hand up when their life is at rock bottom.

Steve, I am so proud to have been part of 56notout and so proud of you.

Julie Atherton May 2019

LOOKING BACK, LOOKING FORWARD

So, it's June 2018, and it's been less than a week since the last day of my challenge year and already I am missing the buzz. We had always planned on taking some time out after the year was over as we, my wife, Julie and I, thought that we would need a holiday. The final few weeks before I turned 57 were manic with the pressure to complete the 56 challenges in my birthday year ever growing as the big day approached. An early start today - up at 2.30am for the first flight out to Mahon, Menorca, the birthplace of mayonnaise and one of our favourite places in the world. After spending a bit of time in the sanctuary of the airport lounge (enjoying the pre-flight G and T's!) the holiday was underway. I am not a nervous flyer, but I always enjoy a little tipple to settle the nerves. Better to be safe than sorry I reckon! Sitting in the *Bar Paput* at the side of the harbour, drinking an ice-cold Estrella from a frosty glass, I was in heaven. As I slipped quickly into holiday mode, I had already started looking back on an incredible year and looking ahead to the future.

How did this all start?

When the 56 Not Out idea was born back in 2016, Friday 2nd December 2016 to be precise, I would never imagine that the year would have had such an impact on my life and those around me.

I can remember sitting on the sofa with a nice glass of red wine - l like a drink or two on a Friday night. I do try not to indulge on a school night but the idea of marking the end of the working week and the arrival of the weekend I feel is definitely something worth celebrating. I didn't know it at the time, but this Friday would be one that I was going to remember. The week had not been particularly different to any other as far as I can recall, except for a passing conversation with one of my longest and closest friends, Nigel Bonas, who was telling me about a colleague of his who was planning a year of challenges to mark a birthday and raise money for charity. The seed was sown and little did I know that the germination time for that passing conversation with Nigel, fuelled with the need to do something, which came earlier on said Friday, combined with a glass or two of Rioja would be shorter than I thought.

Working in the automotive industry, Fridays are traditionally an early finish much to the annoyance of my non-automotive friends who must work a "full week" and is usually the time for me to get a run in with my friend Sue Cox. Today's run through the streets of my hometown Leamington Spa would provide the need to the seedling sown earlier in the week. It was the beginning of December, the countdown to Christmas had started and the winter of 2016 had already begun to make its presence felt. Even though it was early afternoon and still light, the wind provided an icy backdrop to the run. I am not sure why today was different, but I was very conscious of the number of people making the doorways of shops home along with increasing number of folks asking for help. I thought, "this is the 21st century, isn't it? No one today in the so called 'civilised world' we live in should not have a roof over their head, should they?" I ran on to the top of town and the site of swanky "retirement village for the over fifties" to quote the sale pitch with apartments at over 200 thousand pounds a pop and the deal was done. I had my dinner and settled down in front of the TV. Wine was poured and my brain went into overdrive.

I had the idea courtesy of Nigel along with the need highlighted after my afternoon run and the 56 Not Out challenge was born. By the time my wife Julie appeared the following morning to find me still where she had left me several hours earlier with an empty wine bottle, surrounded by paper and an expression on my face that told her that she best sit down and hear what I had to say. I don't think the news that I was about to do something new came as such a shock and her first reaction was how I could possibly take on anything else and a good question, what was I going to give up? "That's the challenge!" I replied with a cheeky grin. But deep down I knew Julie had a point. I barely had time to draw breath as it was, but I knew I would find a way. With my 56th birthday 6 months away, I reckoned that would make a great starting point and 56 challenges seemed like a good enough number - just over one per week. I already had some ideas that would be a bit different to the usual bucket list / fund raising ideas. I gave the bones of the idea and a flavour of some of the ideas on the list to my wife Julie over a cup of tea the following morning. I knew already that this was going to take over our lives and it was important that Julie was with me from the start.

After the initial surprise of seeing me still sat on the sofa where she had said goodnight to me some hours earlier, she was keen to hear what I had to say, initially fearing the worst.

Sharing my passion for the plights of others, Julie had already showed an interest in the work being carried out by local charity, Helping Hands, so she could clearly understand the need. Her obvious concern was how I was ever going to fit anything else in my already full diary; something was going to have to give.

My passion and determination to make the plan happen was clear and I felt that I had her blessing, with a little hesitation, to get the ball rolling. On "the night" in December, I sketched not only the bones of the plan along with some challenge ideas but also some thoughts of a logo and the open words that would kick off the plan to the world. I am pleased that these early words stayed with me for the whole year and were eventually used to announce my plan to the world of social media. They also provided the basis of nearly every letter, email and adhoc conversation with anyone willing to listen. As for the logo ideas I had, more about that later...

Those words: -

"Born from a seed sown by a buddy, the concept is not original but from a passing conversation together with a purpose the 56 Not Out Challenge was born and has started to grow legs.

The number of people living on the streets in our towns and cities is on the increase and I cannot sit back, I need to do something. I am 56 years old this year, not a significant birthday but the need is now. So, as I enter my 56th year on the 30th May 2017 the challenge starts. 56 challenges before I turn 57. Not all the challenges are physical, some will test my powers of persuasion, some my nerve, others will challenge my sanity. To see fair play and keep me on the straight and narrow, my wife Julie will be manning "basecamp" and sharing the journey with me.

I plan to keep my supporters up to date using a blog and social media and engaging help and support for some of the challenges although for many, unfortunately I will be on my own.

The aim of the challenge would be to raise awareness of the issue and what we can do to help along with raising some much-needed funds for a local charity."

Looking back at my journal and reading the entries made around those initial few days you can clearly sense my excitement and the passion starting to build but also a clear acknowledgment that it was not going to be an easy ride. I would have to clear the decks if I stood any chance of pulling this off.

The name of Nigel's friend, who had sown the seed, would remain anonymous for some months to come, but a twist of fate and misfortune would put us in contact with each other later in the challenge year and adding another idea to the growing list and a chance to thank him in person.

I planned to go public at the beginning of May thinking maybe a big launch party but was I letting the idea runaway with itself!

An idea without a plan is just a dream!

A phrase my manager uses a lot in the office but according to the internet, the actual quote is:

"a dream without a plan is just a wish" credited to Katherine Paterson, Chinese-born American writer best known for children's novels including The Invisible Child.

I feel that never a truer statement and as 2016 started to draw to an end, I already had started to develop a sense of urgency. I knew the first few months of a New Year would be over in a flash and the 56notout challenge would dominate the planning for the year ahead.

I was keen to get a logo sorted, to give the idea an identity and Sue, a great friend and my running buddy on that Friday was my starting point. As an accomplished graphic designer, she was the obvious person to talk to and appropriate that Sue was part of the concept as she was there from the very first day. Sue was always there to provide artist support and a later a challenge too but more about that later. Looking back at my original ideas, I can see I was trying to be far too clever. The final design was perfect, a play on the Heinz 57 design along with a tweak to the slogan. A distinctive image would make all the difference and help promote the challenge in the months to come and what became a natural symbol and familiar spectacle especially on race days during the next few months.

The first few months of 2017 were testing times in the Atherton camp, February threw one of many curved balls that would dominate a good proportion of the year but how we would deal with these challenges is what makes us strong, no one said it would be easy!

I had done some fundraising a few times before, but this was different, a much bigger scale and I was realistic that I was a nobody, so to think I was going to get support from the big boys was going to be tough and in hindsight would have needed a lot more time. An impromptu visit to a local printer, ARM, my running groups T-shirt provider for some club merchandise and taking advantage of a new ear to hear my story, I was delighted with the offer of help and support from Stuart and the crew. Some good news after a week of hospital visiting and chippy teas.

With launch day, only a couple of months away I still needed to link up with a charity or better still two to provide a home for all the money I was going to raise. Julie had mentioned Helping Hands several times before and had been following the local charity based in Leamington on social media and was really impressed with the support they were giving people in my hometown, so after checking them out for myself I made contact ....

Hi Lianne,

Following on from my message via Facebook I have hatched a plan to keep me busy in 2017/2018

I have called the idea the 56 Not Out Challenge

Born from a seed sown by a buddy, the concept is not original but from a passing conversation together with a purpose the 56 Not Out Challenge was born and has started to grow legs.

The number of people living on the streets in our towns and cities is on the increase and I cannot sit back, I need to do something. I am 56 years old this year, not a significant birthday but the need is now. So, as I enter my 56th year on the 30th May 2017 the challenge starts. 56 challenges before I turn 57. Not all the challenges are physical, some will test my powers of persuasion, some my nerve, others will challenge my sanity. To see fair play .... etc. etc.

I then went on to list a few of the wacky ideas that I had....

The reply back from Lianne confirmed that Helping Hands were the right choice for our local charity and from the response we realised that this relationship would work well for all of us, with immediate offers some challenge opportunities that Helping Hands could help with.

Hi, Steve!

What a great email to receive! You've got our attention and we are smiling! :)

This sounds absolutely fantastic and thank you so much for considering Helping Hands to raise funds for and help you achieve your 56 challenges!!

We can certainly help you achieve some of these too!! ...we are hoping to have an annual charity fundraising dinner this year and we have only just started putting a team together to help make that happens. You'd be more than welcome to join the events team?

We also have our annual sleep out fundraiser in November again this year, so definitely, we would love you get involved in that-last year we raised £13k..it was very cold and rainy :(

We are joining in the 100-miler cycle ride (other smaller miles available 35/65) in September for the Warwickshire for the wiggle tempest-you're more than welcome to sign up to our group.

We can also have you come along to our soup kitchen for sure! :)

This is such a fantastic idea and we have quite a few contacts who will spread the word and make all these a possibility for you.

We would definitely love to be involved in this amazing fun 56 challenge and more than happy to be associated with it!

We look forward to following all your progress! Well done! Amazing! And thank you for following our work :)

I'll look forward to updates.

Lianne

I could tell from Lianne's response that the challenge idea was something different to the usual fundraising activities that she usually came across and I had definitely caught her attention. At that moment, I hoped that this response would become the norm but only time would tell. I was really keen that the 56notout challenge was not perceived as my own bucket list and an opportunity for me to do a load of fun stuff in the name of fundraising. Each and every challenge had to have a clear reason to be on the list. As I let you know more about the challenges in the pages of this book, I will attempt to explain more about the background behind them. With the challenge year over, I will also share the challenges that never made the final 56 and why but before I look back, I need to look ahead.

Time to spread my wings

I had my local charity on board, but as I hoped interest in the challenge would make it further than my home county of Warwickshire, I thought a second national charity would be a good idea. Figuring that if I was to engage more people in the plight of the homeless, the connection to just a local charity might limit the interest. With the challenge in mind, I had already entered the London Marathon ballot earlier in the year, with one of my challenges to run a marathon. If you are going to run 26.2 miles, the only place to do this to be honest is London. Unfortunately, the chances are getting a ballot place are pretty slim and I knew with my limited running ability I had very little chance of a "good for age" place awarded to runners who had run pre-determined distances in good times. With my times I was more likely to be offered a place on a trip to outer space so having done some research into which charities offered places, Shelter was the obvious choice. I applied for a place with them. Even before the challenge started, I had to use all my powers of persuasion to convince Shelter that I could raise the £2000 required to secure the place. Considering that I had already committed to share all donations between the two charities, the task instantly became twice as difficult as the fund-raising target becoming £4000. A big task in these times where money is tight. I liked the idea that fundraising occasionally gave people something when they parted with the cash like a product or an experience but also keeping the issues facing the homeless at the top of the agenda.

Raising awareness, however, was the most important part of the challenge in my eyes, I thought it was time to go back to school.

I didn't actual go back to school, but I needed to learn some new skills that would help in the weeks and months ahead.

Having already made a commitment in my opening words to the world, that I would be doing a weekly blog. However, what I knew about blogging you could write on the back of a cigarette packet, so I need help. Some years ago, I was involved with a great charity call Kids Run Free which was a brilliant initiative to get kids into regular exercise for free and this was based in my hometown. Kids Run Free was launched in 2010 as the personal project of lifelong friends and competitive athletes Martine Verweij and Catherine O'Carroll. The ladies were already owners of a successful sport management company called Raceways and had attended many running events where children watched adults take part but they had no opportunity to participate themselves. They saw a need to create opportunities that would inspire kids to run and wanted to use their own events to provide this and so the initiative call Kids Run Free was born. I became familiar with the concept and with Martine and Catherine initially through the regular, monthly Saturday morning sessions with my daughters and later getting more involved and becoming race director in 2011 for the local group in Leamington. Here I got to know some of the parents and the children really well. One of the dads was a chap called Chris Spriggs. I liked the Spriggs family. I liked the passion and enthusiasm that they brought to the game along with the true values of life that Chris was clearly imparting on his children. Sometime after we met, Chris embarked on a challenge of his own. To push his uncle Andrew who was diagnosed with motor neurone disease, in a wheelchair in the Brighton Marathon. I had limited experience of running from pushing the wheelchair of the late and great Judy Wolfenden OBE. I first met the legendary, if a little eccentric, fund raiser back in 2011 when I responded to Judy's appeal for runners in the local newspaper to push her wheelchair in the annual hundred mile Cotswold Ultra event in June of the same year. Running in relay, teams pushed Judy overnight to cross the finish line sometime the following evening braving all weathers to raise money for lesser known charities. This was the first of a number of events with Judy before her sad death two years later in 2013.

Over a coffee, I passed on some of the tips I had learnt the hard way from pushing Judy in her high-tech chair that would help Chris on his mission to push his uncle in the months ahead. I began to follow his exploits via his weekly blog, and little did I know that I would feature in his writings in the months to come. Chris was the perfect person to talk to as I do like to multi-task and I also like the idea of a run and a natter as a perfect opportunity to pick his brains. The fresh air was nice too. Choosing Stratford park run as a local venue, which would be significant later in the challenge year when Chris and I would meet again, but you will have to wait a while to find out more.

We ran we chatted and by the end of the three laps of the riverside park I knew far more about blogging than I did 5k earlier. Chris's blog *"Think Smile Run"* became the making of the book *"The reason I run"* and I was thrilled to have my own chapter.

I had planned to post my blog at the weekend with the first post on the 1st May 2017 - 30 days before the challenge year started and my eagerly awaited 56th birthday. Short and sweet with just enough detail to set the scene of what I was about to take on and engage some early interest.

The first blog :-

1st May 2017 - Go hard or go home

Today is the day, 30 days until the 56 Not Out challenge starts on 30 May 2017. 56 challenges in 365 days to help raise awareness and much needed funds to help the homeless, the final planning is well underway and just adding the final touches. I am still short of a few ideas and would appreciate any suggestions, nothing too tough on this poor old body of mine.

If you want to get involved or just want to give your support, then get on board. It's going to be fun as well as tough. Throughout the year I will be asking for help so be warned.

Continuing the learning process, I soon realised that I was lacking in some basic literacy skills so after the first blog went public, I changed the routine. I would draft out the rough words on my laptop then gave it to Julie who turned it in to something vaguely resembling English that made sense - protecting me from the grammar police - but her main role was to keep me on the straight and narrow. As the year progressed, you can clearly tell the blogs that skipped this quality control process, but sometimes I knew what I want to say and just hoped that I didn't commit too many literary faux pas. I know from my professional life that the clarity of the message is everything and your brain can get distracted by the grammar and punctuation leaving the important point missed.

I quickly learned to value the support of others and the team ethos that was developing as the fast approach of the "go live" day and the reality grew ever closer. This support would be crucial if I was going to keep the momentum to take me to my 57th birthday.

The weeks leading up to my birthday were tough in many ways, having gone public, I felt flat almost immediately and I just wanted to get on with it eager to get some challenges under my belt. I have never been a patient person, I am a "now" sort of guy which is one of my worst traits according to my family. I am getting better as I am getting older; I am told.

I knew these first few weeks of the challenge year were vitally important, I needed to start building interest in a way that would engage people to share my journey. This was definitely a marathon and not a sprint and reckoned that the variety side of the concept would help with challenges that would resonate with different people.

Social media is a great tool for spreading the word, but very much an instant forum. In the past when people describe newspaper headline becoming tomorrow's fish and chip paper, Facebook is even more in the moment. The pace that news feeds progress is incredible - miss something and it's gone! However, I soon realised that if you get a dialogue going then the shelf life does extend somewhat. I realised that I was on a massive learning curve and I was going to need help. I am a bit old school to be honest and did not want to rely on just new technology and wanted to use traditional methods that I knew a little more about.

The first breakthrough was when I reached out to the local press, keeping my press release simple and to the point, the challenge idea was clearly different enough to catch the eye of the reporters from both the Observer and the Courier. And so, on the 12th May, I headed down to the Helping Hands Headquarters, the Lighthouse, for the first photo shoot of the campaign.

The first appearance in the paper on the 15th May was a very surreal experience, seeing the picture and reading the words made the challenge so very real. This public commitment made going back on my word impossible; not that I ever had any intention of doing that. Catherine Thompson from the Observer's article summed up my thoughts. Meeting the observer photographer Jon Mullis at the Lighthouse gave me the first of many dealings with the press and little did I know that our paths would continue to cross throughout the next twelve months.

This initial meeting with the press, gave me the first opportunity to show off my new branded 56notout T shirt with the great logo that would feature though out the year.

The article :-

A KIND-HEARTED Warwick man will be taking compassion to a new level as he completes an impressive 56 fundraising challenges for charity.

Steve Atherton is organising his one-man campaign '56 Not Out,' to not only mark his upcoming birthday in good stead, but to raise money for Leamington-based homeless charity Helping Hands.

From performing ten pull-ups and dressing up as a knight, to abseiling and completing 56 runs each with 56 different people – Steve has collectively set himself around 280 challenges.

The 55-year-old dad of two, set himself the gruelling challenge after being shocked at the number of homeless people he passed during a run last winter.

Steve told The Observer: "What really struck me was that there was a homeless person in a doorway of this expensive looking retirement home.

"I didn't sleep all night; I was tearing my hair out. Something needs to change. But I didn't know what, or how."

It was then Steve came across Helping Hands, which runs a drop-in centre, soup kitchen, and schemes to help vulnerable people find accommodation and work.

And with some 800 people registered homeless in Leamington, volunteers and fundraisers are needed more than ever.

Anthony Dwyer from Helping Hands said: "Without volunteers and people like Steve, we couldn't help all the people we do. We are overwhelmed by Steve's efforts and compassion to raise awareness in the wider community. We are 100 per cent behind him and really want him to succeed."

Steve, who is also raising money for national homeless charity Shelter, hopes to raise £2,000 for Helping Hands.

He said: "It's not just about money but about breaking down boundaries and encouraging people to do little things whether it's buying a homeless person a coffee or putting coins in a charity money box."

Steve's first challenge is to take on the Two Castles Run between Warwick and Kenilworth Castle, in a costume yet to be revealed.

Follow Steve's page '56 Not Out' on Facebook to support him and read more about his journey.

The article was reused in Warwick University's newspaper - The Boar, the following month.

Even before I tackled my first challenge, I found an increasing awareness of the world around me. I like to think that I am not a shallow person and have a little depth to my personality and thoughts but already I had started to look at life and the people I was starting to come in contact with in completely different ways.

Nothing is forever and depending on your views we only pass this way but once. I feel it's the right time for me to try and make a difference. Having my family with me on the journey was important as I knew that the year would impact them too. Many will have an opinion as to how well I cope with attention and being at the centre of the action and to be honest, I am not sure myself. My confidence has grown over the years and poles apart from the person of my childhood, an observation that would be made later in the year from an old junior school classmate. Even in these early weeks, the seeds were being sown for ideas that would involve every member of the family. I liked having support when I am in public but I know not everyone likes being centre of attention and that I had to continue to respect having someone watch my back and also getting a different perspective on what was going on is a very healthy element of the challenge year. I planned from time to time to let go of the reins and let you read the words of others.

Not really sure of the connection to subject but my late parents are never far away from my thoughts. My dad was a complicated character, a person with an amazing sense of humour, but not someone as you would describe as a great leader. But the older I get and the more I think about him; I am now not so sure. I can see that he didn't need to be at the front to demonstrate his leadership skills but leading from within. A story and food for thought.

A group of wolves: the three in front are old and sick, they walk in front to set the pace lest they get left behind. The next five are the strongest and the best, they are tasked to protect the front side if there is an attack. The pack in the middle are always protected from any attack. The five behind them are also amongst the strongest and the best, they are to protect the back side of the group if there is an attack. The wolf at the back is the leader. He keeps the pack unified and on the same path. He is always ready to run in any direction to protect and serves as the bodyguard to the entire group. Being a leader is not about being at the front, it's about taking care of the whole pack.

I think my dad had learnt that life skill, maybe during his time in the navy and subconsciously or maybe intentionally, used this as part of the way he led his life. I will never know but as the challenges progressed, I was caused to look into my own life and my own journey. My father, Ron, spent his working life on the newspapers and the support from his final employer who published the Leamington Courier and felt a connection with the local paper thanks to Kirsty Smith, one of the reporters who played and continues to support the challenge.

My mum, my *amazing* mum was the most social person I have ever met. She loved people and everyone knew Rose. My great mate Allan loved my mum as much as his own mother and even to this day rarely a conversation about our youth goes by without a reference to my mum. She was very much a part of my gang as we grew up and my mates thought the world of her. Famous for the post lads' night out breakfast, a runny egg, just what we needed after a belly full of beer; but I loved the part she played in my childhood. Her life ended ridiculously too soon at the age of 64 and felt she missed the later years of my own life, having never got to see her granddaughters, although I feel that she is never far from me or my thoughts and still remains a massive part of the person I am today. I am sure my mum would have loved being part of the crazy if a little dysfunctional family that we have today.

12th May 2017 - Carpe Diem – Seize the day

This phrase has come up a lot this week, a busy week, a sad week and inspiring week. Meeting Lianne and the team at Helping Hands filled both Julie and I with hope for this crazy planet of ours. Even before the challenge kicks off the money has started to come in and for that I thank you. The challenge was never about the money, I was always confident that would happen, but I wanted to learn more about how to help and the process has already started. I will share all this great information with you, so we can learn together. One of the challenges that I am looking forward to is running with 56 different people and today I met Mark, who is getting his life together and very much looking forward to hearing his story and getting to know this guy.

I have had a couple of new challenges too, a lovely arty one, which will result hopefully in a calendar to put in your Christmas stocking (thank you Sue) and my wife Julie wants to be a scare crow and stand in a field – no tech, no headphones, just the birds! (I think she wants me to slow down sometimes) so I may appear in a field near you…

I had the pleasure of seeing the musical Rent – hard hitting and very relevant.

> *Five hundred twenty-five thousand six hundred minutes*
> *How do you measure a year?*
> *In daylights, in sunsets*
> *In midnights, in cups of coffee*
> *In inches, in miles*
> *In laughter, in strife*
> *Season in Love*

What happened this week to get under my skin, my weekly blog clearly points to something, what was it? Looking back at my old journal, the clue was there.

From the start I wanted to play with a straight bat to keep some credibility to the whole challenge. I was delighted to have the opportunity to go on the radio, but Saturday 20th May, that was a few days ahead of the challenge start date, appearing on the radio was on the list but 56 challenges in the birthday year. No way could I count it but I need not have worried as help was at hand and being on the radio would not be a problem in fact, I ended up on three maybe even four different radio stations numerous times during the year and one of the presenters became a good friend and one of my 56 runners!

The first appearance was very special, when the invitation came into my inbox from Sarah James, weekend programming at BBC Coventry and Warwickshire. I was thrilled, excited and nervous all at the same time. I was amazed how the word got around in those first few weeks and I had to call Sarah to confirm my attendance and to give her more background information that would help the presenter on the day. I had never been on the radio before and did not know what to expect. Arriving at the Coventry City Centre studio, the first thing that surprised me was the security. I do understand why but was nevertheless it was unexpected. Once in the studio, the atmosphere was really relaxing, and I loved the technology. The Saturday morning presenter, Lorna Bailey, was lovely and immediately made me feel at ease. We had a mutual friend, Guy Jackson, and even got him a mention on air. With Julie by my side and nice cup of coffee, Lorna and I chatted like we had known each other for years, albeit going out live across Warwickshire. With the offer to return visit mid challenge, I made note of the mistakes and missed opportunities, good learning ready for next time.

A different experience with Free Radio, when I did a telephone interview that was edited and broadcast on air later in the week - I am sure that counted didn't it? But would depend on when it went out, trust my luck it will go out too early...

But what got under my skin? As Julie and I walked from the car park through the quieter back waters of Coventry, the darker more secluded corners of the grounds of the old priory had become home to several of the cities increasing number of rough sleepers. The early morning image of someone cocooned in a lonely solitary world reinforced the need to do something and ahead of my debut appearance on the radio, if I needed any more motivation to take on this crazy year, then this was it.

21st May 2017 - Every day's a school day

This week has been very much a time for learning, I always knew that it would not be easy once I started looking into the grey side of life but for too many this is reality, that it would be tough. Not every problem has a black and white solution as I know from my day job, the answer is not always popular and the issues that many faced are complicated. Even before the challenge starts, I am in awe of the people who work so selflessly to help make a difference for those who need support in our towns and cities. I have also seen them criticised for the way they do things, seems like everyone has their opinion, sometimes we forget that these heroes are humans too and have their own busy lives, other jobs, families and problems like the rest of us to deal with.

As the start day of the challenge gets every closer, I just want to get going now.

I am still having challenges given to me, how about this – "shake the hand of the prime minister" – best get one elected first......

WINDOWS OF OPPORTUNITY

A strange series of events, an introduction and windows of opportunity and is if it was meant to be…

I found myself at Leamington Cricket Club and an evening with Gary McKee, a legendary runner and leading fundraiser for McMillan in memory of his late father, who died from cancer and inspired Gary to do many amazing things, including running 100 marathons in 100 days. Running one is a struggle for the average person and not what the body was built for but 100, day after day for three months, now that's an achievement. Sue could not attend the talk tonight, but had heard Gary talk before and recommended the night and also introduced me to her friend Catherine Williamson played host to Gary on his regular visits to the Royal borough. Before I knew it, I was chatting in a quiet corner with Gary and was an inspiration even before I took my seat with Kieron and listened to his life's story. The advice given to me in our short conversation would stand me in great shape for the rest of the challenge year along with the promise to be one of my 56 runners.

Gary was straight to the point with his questions and advice. I knew he was talking from experience and the heart; his passion was infectious. "Are you married, Steve? Get your misses to deal with all your admin, you leave all the bookings and arrangements to her and just focus on the challenges, you will have enough to do. Got kids? Social media, leave it to a younger member of the family, you're too old mate. The youth live and breathe Facebook and will get your name out there" and so with the advice from a pro, I intently listened to Gary and hope one day to take to the public speaking circuit, Catherine might be part of that dream, watch this space.

The night was very balanced, three speakers, Gary Mankini, Gary McKee's childhood friend and complete loon, Michelle McGagh, "the no spend year" who spoke about living with next to nothing, a frugal life and the main man Gary Mckee of course. Gary's cumbrian accent and down to earth talking was great to hear and loved that it was stat free and untechnical, a few beers and a curry the night before the London Marathon, my sort of runner. I am full of respect for this man, a great rounded evening and left looking forward to running with him as the year progressed.

The next few days, taking on board Gary's words of wisdom, Julie and Emma officially joined team 56notout and the rest is history.

LET'S DO THIS

At last the day has arrived. 30th May 2017. Cometh the hour, cometh the man! After all the anticipation, it started pretty much as normal. Julie and I had started early morning swimming sessions at a local school. Knowing that water was a big fear of mine and I knew it would feature at some point in the list of challenges, Julie suggest that I get as much time in the water as I could, what did she know that I didn't? I am not a great swimmer, never have been. I can swim but the breaststroke and a poor imitation of a back stroke with the only similarity being that I face upwards being the limit of my aquatic repertoire. Julie however is a good swimmer, I hoped she would help me improve my technique just in case I need to push myself but soon realised that I was beyond help although between sniggers, she did impart a modicum of her knowledge and I do feel I am the better for it. Time will tell....

It was a chilly morning even though it was early but expected it to be a little warmer being May but nevertheless, I did take time out to record a video. Partly to use the backdrop of skeletal rugby players in full flight as a symbolic start to the challenge and also provided some thing to do whilst waiting for Julie to appear from the sports centre. So, I have done it, my first video on the Facebook page and no going back now but to be honest and in the words of Gene Kranz - Apollo Flight Director "failure was not an option". Just for the record, he never actual said that and was a product of the film industry but who cares.

My workday was pretty much the same as any other except for cakes. The folks in my office favour samosas but I am a bit of a traditionalist, so donuts, muffins and cookies were the order of the day, after all it was my birthday.

RUN #1 — SUSAN COX

The first challenge to start and would end up carrying on until the closing hours of the last day of my mammoth year was to run with 56 different people. It seems right that #1 should be Sue, she was there at the challenge birth and had already played a big part in the preparation. Sue came to our house after work and arrived bearing gifts, a birthday present that I would soon realise was a simple but thoughtful gift. A journal for all my runners to add their names and words of wisdom to pages of a book blazoned with of course the 56notout logo. I loved the journal. Sue had already christened the first page which many others would follow as the year progressed. Julie took a phone video to mark the occasion as we headed off for the inaugural run. We talked of the year ahead and the many challenges that were to come and if I would ever get to run with Daniel Craig......

The plan was in its infancy and on the first of the early runs, photos would provide the evidence along with a reminder if I need a prompt or two but I did not introduce the on-run video, that came a little later and to this day my friend Steve mentioned that he missed out on the media attention at any opportunity.

After our run around historic Warwick, my hometown, it was back for a shower and out for a curry with the family along a rousing rendition of happy birthday and a birthday cake with the logo. I soon realised that I would be seeing a lot of that shield before the year would be over. Little did I know that one of my challenges to be on the radio could already be ticked off the list as Freeradio had aired a pre-recorded interview on the teatime "drive time" show whilst I was out for a run with Sue. I had already been on the radio the weekend before as I have already mentioned, but the challenge hadn't started yet so was reluctant to count it, but I need not have worried as I made the first of my many of radio appearances on my birthday, that was one in the bag - result!

I reckoned that if this year was going to work, I should aim to get at least a challenge a week done along with a run with someone at the same frequency and a city a month know that I could occasional get a double hit if I could run with someone in a different city.

Day 1, first runner and first challenge in the bag, piece of cake this....

3rd June 2017 - Let's do this!

So, I am officially another year older and the talking stops, it's now time to do the doing! Tuesday was emotional and the first challenge to run with 56 different people started when I had the pleasure to run with my great friend and talented graphic designer Sue Cox who I can thank for the great "56notout" logo which seems to be appearing on everything from a lovely birthday card, running journal (be prepared to sign it folks if you run with me) and my cake too. I made it onto the radio on my birthday, so I can officially tick off at least one challenge. I have secured my place in the 2018 London Marathon and bought myself a pair of speedos now that I am going to have to take this swimming lark seriously!

What brought the reason I'm doing this home was when today, I was stopped in the street and asked for money and I did not know how to respond except shrugging my shoulders and walking away. This is the last time I will do this; I want to do the right thing and want to share my learning with you.

A busy work week ahead and a manic weekend at the end of it with my guest appearance on Warwick Market selling fruit and veg on Saturday and of course the big reveal of my Two Castles outfit Sunday - come and say hello if you can!

I appreciate each and every one of you who has talked to me, followed the Facebook page, read the blog and parted with hard earned cash — thank you.

I cannot do this without you!

CITY #1 – GOTHENBURG

At the end of the first week, I felt great with one challenge done and runners queuing up. I thought this was going to be a doddle, but I should not have counted my chickens just yet. Life does have a happy knack of throwing a curved ball or two as I was soon to fine out.

Looking back at my journal, I noted that I was already feeling the pressure. I had already blocked in some key dates in the plan along with some challenges I wanted to do, one being to run in 10 cities the other to run with 56 different people. Doing the maths, to stay on plan every week I would have to complete at least one challenge, run with a new person as well as a city once a month plus be a husband, dad and keep down a full-time job. What had I let myself in for?

Week 2 was shaping up well too with more challenges lined up for the weekend and my job would take me to Sweden and a chance to run in the first of ten cities, Gothenburg. One of my favourite cities in the world and a great place to run. Since my last visit, the engineering team had relocated from within the manufacturing plant to a harbour side office block in city suburb of Eriksberg on the northern banks of the river Göta Älv and pretty much in the heart of the city. Our hotel was next to the office, in the same block so a great location and a very easy commute to work. This regenerated side of the city once a thriving area for ship building is dominated by the 84-metre-high gantry crane, the Eriksberg Crane, bright red and standing as a remnant the areas ship building past. Running along the wide riverside paths, with busy waterways on one side and classy boutiques, swanky apartments and offices plus inviting restaurants serving the promise of local seafood, I had plenty to take my mind off the miles. As I ran, the crane was always in my eye-line and so before heading back to my hotel for a shower and a chance to enjoy a lovely dinner, I had to take a detour to the iconic crane and soon stood in awe at the base of one it's mighty wheeled feet. I stood with bright eyed and mouth wide open looking up at the beast towering above me which seemed to have a personality all of its own. A dramatic and imposing landmark of the city and after my colleagues and I had eaten, I returned with Thomas, Robert and Jeff for a second look and all were equally overwhelmed. Just for the record, dinner was pretty good too.

With the work week over and back in my own bed I had a busy weekend ahead. I love my hometown of Warwick and my life is full of little routines and habits. If my ongoing project of writing a book called "Running off at a Tangent" ever sees the light of day you will find out a lot more about them but for now I need to stay focused on getting the 56notout story down on paper so for now you will have to just know that one of my little Saturday routines is to have a three or four mile run around my local park, over the bridge to check out the best view of Warwick Castle into town, through the market square passing all the stall holders setting up shop for the weekly market and home via another hidden gem of Warwick, Priory Park. Since living in Warwick, on returning home and having showered the effects of my exercise away and changed into something less fitness based, we usually headed back into town by car to have a stroll around the market and stocking up fruit and vegetables for the week ahead. Ok they sell the usual imported goodies but generally what is best is what is in season. A few weeks before I had explained the usual pleasantries with our regular stall then casually asked who the boss was and when Shane said it was him, I plunged a letter in his hand and said, "read this, I'll be back next week".

The letter of course was introducing the challenge and asking if they would take me on for the day later in the year.

He read it there and then and said, "no problem buddy, happy to help" immediately introducing me to Sam, Nat and the rest of the team. "Steve's going to come and work for us" and so I explained what was going on and why they had some middle-aged man thrust upon them. Immediately I felt at ease with these folks and although their Leicester accents proved a little tricky to understand at first, I knew I would be in safe hands. It had been a few weeks since we agreed a date but came around very quickly and really happy that if the plan came off, I would get two challenges completed in the first two weeks. A great confidence boost if I was going to sustain this pressure that I had put the team and I under.

Working on the market would help in many ways I thought, I am not a wall flower but if this year was going to do what I wanted, I had to up my game and create interest in what I was doing and raise awareness of the amazing work these charities were doing. Gaining trust of relative strangers was going to be a key feature of the year and many times, my trust in others. The day was an early start but instead of my usual early morning run, I dressed for work and walked the short distance to the square in time for set up. Shane put me with Sam whose knowledge of the trade far exceeded her years. I spend my working life, sat on my backside in a comfortable air-conditioned office. My hands are soft and smooth but today I was going to have to graft. Laying out the grass, the artificial type that the produce would be displayed on was the first job, turning the stark wooden market tables into a country garden and providing a soft backdrop to the fruit and veg. You buy with your eyes and not a hint of cling film or packaging in site. Laying out the greens was good fun, then came the humping. Sacks of this, trays of that. Soon the stall looked brilliant, ready for business and I was knackered already. I had been on my feet an hour already and not had a cuppa yet. I had a plan; I will keep the stalls stocked up as the great and the good of Warwick came to buy the goodies on offer and I would leave the selling to the old pros. My plan some went out the window as the customers started coming thick and fast, I had no choice "Good Morning Madam, how can I help you" and I was a market trader. As for the scales, I could live to a hundred and not get the hang of that bit of kit. The others made it look like child's play but to me, I was way outside my comfort zone already. As my friends started to show up, I had to look like I knew what I was doing. The team had already posted on social media to come and check my lovely plums and that about set the tone. By nine a clock, I was in my element, but my legs were starting to ache, and the offer of a coffee and a pasty was very welcome. Little did I know it would take me the best part of 45 minutes to eat as no sooner that I took a bite, a customer appeared. "Good morning madam, shall I take those from you, some carrots no problem. We have run a little low, let me open you a fresh sack." How was I supposed to know that those were for horses, sorry people of Warwick, a carrot is a carrot? A mistake is only a mistake if you do it twice, I was also told. I was glad of moral support as friends and family popped by to see me in action knowing that the word would soon spread and photographs appearing on Facebook. I was having a good time, but this was not just about fun. When customers were buying a single potato, three sprouts and a carrot, I knew they were not planning a lavish dinner party. This was definitely a meal for one and guessed this would be the only human interaction that some might see today. Nat whispered in my ear, "only charge her a pound, Steve, she does not have a lot of money." I was touched, charity ready does begin at home, I liked this.

Serving Julie our usual goodies from the other side of the counter was a little surreal and walking her to the car made a welcome break from the constant flow of customers and looked forward to returning home later and putting my feet up.

Having spent what felt like the longest day ever on my feet, that was probably not the best preparation for Challenge number 3 which was the next morning, run 10k in fancy dress.

But what should I wear?

I went out to my growing group of supporters for ideas what I could wear for my debut appearance running in fancy dress. Nothing offensive, no excess of flesh and suitably for running six undulating miles mostly up hill. The ideas came thick and fast but when Kate Shaw responded on social media with comment - "surely it's got to be a bottle of ketchup hasn't it? I knew she was right. Julie was on the internet and soon the now famous red costume arrived in the post. Sue arranged the logo to be printed at ARM, the local printing company that had already become the teams' supplier of all thing's logo based. Stuart sprung to action and the logo was ready to be added to the outfit. My sewing and costume designing skills end at replacing a button, so the extended team came to the rescue. Sue's mum adapting the front and my youngest daughter Millie, making the final adjustments to the bottle itself to make it comfortable to wear, with that and the arrival of the big day, I was ready.

The annual Two Castles, a run between the magnificent castle in Warwick, built in 1068 to the ruins of the 13th century castle in Kenilworth and attracts both club runners, fun runners and joggers alike. You do see the odd fancy dress outfit, but these usually take the form of a tutu or a pair of fairy wings. Red tights had been purchased to accompany the ketchup out fit and putting those on should have been a challenge all on its own. Flexibility is not one of my strongest attributes, I got the one foot in ok but how the bloody hell could I bend in two to introduce the other foot. I needed a woman to show me the way and soon I was looking like an extra in a Christmas film. I decided to dress modestly but minimalist under the bottle as I knew the nature of the fabric was not of a breathable type and soon, I would be sweating like a Geordie at a spelling test. Sue and I were dropped off near the entrance to the start, choosing a quiet back street to slip into the outfit and emerging to a busy West Street to introduce the world to ketchup man! The looks started straight away and soon developed into a smile. The start set up different this year with the organisers opting to keep the sport club runners away from us athletes so almost immediately on entering the castle ground, Sue and I went our separate ways. Trying to blend in and failing miserably, I walked through the Peacock Garden and into the Central Courtyard. I had planned to meet the rest of the zero to hero group, our little Run England running gang, but I was a little early but soon meeting people I knew I did not feel so self-conscious. I have never run in fancy dress before and was not sure how others would respond. To run 10k for many people is a big deal and train religiously to be ready for the event, I certainly did not want to belittle the effort of what I always refer to as real runners. Club runners are different to the average Joe, always chasing their personal bests and focused for sure. Do these folks ever enjoy the journey or is it's always about the end, the result? Controversial maybe but I always relate to the average man or woman in the street saying, I'm going to do the Two Castles and putting in the work to complete this iconic race never going to win but at the end wearing the medal with pride along with a smile.

Arriving at the meeting point in the shadow of Caesar's Tower, I had already seen a few people I know and trying to look cool but failing miserably to do so but attention, which was the name of the game had already started to work. I had not expected totally strangers asking for a Selfie with me, but I had better get used to this. One of the many people I bumped into was Ellen and Maggie, both regulars at the local park runs and I have always been full of admiration of Maggie, who had been blind since birth and Ellen, her selfless guide and hearing her provide the visual commentary of who I was, what I was wearing and why was brilliant. Little did I know that both ladies would play a significant role in the year ahead.

The race start time approached and with the gang assembled, we made our way to the line. A big turnout today with 4000 runners eager to start and head off to the neighbouring town of Kenilworth and the finish. With the muffled waffle of the local dignitaries rambling on, killing time before the welcome sound of the horn and the off. The mass bopped and shuffled as the start came into sight and with watches poised, we were off. Emerging out of the shady east gate of the castle and spilling onto the closed streets of Warwick, the spectacle always attracts a good crowd near the start with the clapping and cheering a welcome incentive to run. With such a big field and with the race only just underway, the pack grouped together like a sprawling tide of bodies all eager to get ahead of the masses and find some space. Staying together as a group with this many people is almost impossible but for once the additional height of the bottle helped. I always encourage people to run their own race and do the best you can, which is code for "don't wait for me, I can't run that fast!" Anne, one of my regular dawn runners and a lot quicker than me had other ideas. She was having way too much fun with me and stuck to my side the whole run. The smile on her face did nothing to hide the fact that she was having a ball. The first half a mile or so was relatively flat as the route winds its way out of town and then the first hill, a gradual incline with a balanced decent from the top. Julie and her friend Laura had arranged to wait just after the top. An easy place to see the red outfit coming over the brow of the hill and a nice down to add to the pace. I always love to see familiar faces on route and today was no exception. A short stop for photos and away, the crowds thinned out as the run progressed into no man's land between Warwick and the pretty village of Leek Wooten where nearly every inhabitant stands at the end of their drives and cheers, many with bowls of jelly babies, food of the gods for us runners and always appreciated. Taking the sharp left in the village though my favourite part of the route, a shallow decent followed by a gentle climb though a tree lined tunnel giving cooling shade and a chance to drop the headpiece and allowing my already sweat soaked hair to cool off. Anne, my self-appointed wing man, could see that I was getting warm, the red glow of my face a real give away. "You ok" she asked in that all too familiar Michigan accent. Although living in England on and off since 1996, the accent still as strong as ever but with and English twang. With most of the countryside miles complete and the last big hill in sight, familiar faces from David and Sue and a welcome water station, much need refreshment before the climb into Kenilworth. Always a popular cheering point, inevitably a camera or two to capture the fight for breath on the way up to the top. Always some I know around this point and sure enough, the Roberts and the Robertson's in their usual places. Thanks folks means a lot to have your support. From the top of Rouncil Lane, I always feel that the race is nearly over but in fact still another couple of kilometres to go. More cheering and more familiar faces, "ketchup!" was becoming the all too familiar chant or "come on you saucy bugger" another favourite. The best was to come but you are going to have to wait a few months to hear what that was. With Anne still by my side as my much-needed wingman, we could hear the finish in the distance and running out of Brookside Avenue and on to Borrowell Lane the crowds were three deep and the support went up a level. More familiar faces and more hills, the first more welcome than the latter but we are nearly done. Another challenge complete and I knew what it felt like to be different. Off to the Virgin and Castle pub to meet the heroes for a welcome cuppa and a sit down along with a chance to take off the hot suit and cool down a little. Back to looking like a pantomime extra in my red tights. With the arrival of the bacon sandwiches came the obvious comment "does anyone want any ketchup?"

The knock on the door later in the day, with Ray Morgan delivering a surprise from the Rotary Club of Kenilworth, the award for best fancy dress was the icing on the cake on such a great day. And on plan so far....

11th June 2017 - A warm glow...

What a week hence why I am a day late for my weekly blog! As predicted, very busy on the work and home front along with the country as whole and I am learning that not every problem has an easy solution. Having ran in a city, Gothenburg, earlier in the week, a tenth of one challenge it was nice to tick another couple off the list this weekend, but this is never been about a bucket list or playing the numbers. The last couple of days has given me a warm glow and restored my faith in human nature. Working on Warwick market with Shane, Jan, Jan, Sam, Nat and the rest of the crew on the best fruit and veg stall ever gave me an insight into man helping fellow man, very touching and a few quid in the pot for the charities too. Bloody hard work and I take my hat off to these folks, thank you to everyone who came along and said hello, lovely to spread the word. Today the warm came from both within and from the great folks of Warwickshire. It was very hot in that outfit but worth it to see Facebook glowing with support and interest in the campaign. Three challenges done, fifty-three to go, really appreciate you sharing my journey – thankyou. What's next asked the man...... watch this space.

Run #2 – Kieron Carvell

By coincidence, the second person I had the pleasure to run with was the person who got me into running in the first place. I am not a natural runner; at school, sport was to be avoided and most weeks when games came around on the school timetable I arrived at school armed with a note from my mum, anything to get me out of anything remotely physical but late in life I discovered that I actually liked sport. I dabbled with squash back in the Eighties like most men of a certain age will remember and I have always enjoyed the gym but not running, this came to me with the help and support of Kieron I discovered that putting on the trainers and hitting the streets was good fun so I started running back in 2004 with my first race the following spring. Building from short distances at first to eventuality taking on a marathon some years later, for my fiftieth birthday to be precise when the family and I headed to foreign lands of Scotland to run the 26.2 miles in Edinburgh. I have known Kieron since working together on the Jaguar X type at Whitley Engineering Centre in Coventry way back in the late nineties together we have shared many adventures over the years, either in walking boots, in trainers and on the odd occasion, on two wheels along with the odd curry or two, but today was all about the run and with a date in the diary, Kieron suggested a meeting point in the car park of Kenilworth Castle unaware of the significance of the location and the route that we followed until after we had finished. On route, we chatted and reminisced about the past along with debating life and it's meaning as you do. I had given him the heads up that I had a running journal for him to add some words of wisdom into at the end of the run and he was prepared. I could tell that a lot of thought had gone into not only the words he wrote in my black book but also the route we had run. Kieron keeps a running log and tonight we retraced the route of the first time I ever ran 10k back in 2005.

We took the photo at the end, the video was yet to feature as part of the running ritual, that didn't happen until four runners in, but the simple words Kieron wrote in my journal with reference to the significance of the route made it special and reinforced the impact of the journey that I had embarked on.

Re-run of our first 10k run in training for the 2005 Two Castles. Proud to be part of Steve's running journey from Zero to Hero.

Run #3 – Steve Child

Hot on the heels of Kieron came run #3 with Steve Child, I was worried about running with this man. This guy is an athlete, he wins things and everything so the thought of running along with Steve fighting for my breathe as I tried to keep up did worry me ever so slightly. I see him out on his training runs sometimes on the way to work looking every bit of a well-oiled machine, head up and in the groove. Even as I drove from home to collect some bread from my local bakers, Crustums, to have with my avocado and poached eggs, post run, (a bit of a favourite breakfast on a weekend) I passed Steve heading down the road in the opposite direction pumping like an express train. I thought we were having a run but this was Steve's pre run training run. Once I had bought my bread and retraced my journey pulling into the Warwickshire gym car park, my running companion headed in from the opposite direction looking like he had just come out the house, fresh as a daisy. I have known Steve since we worked on a secret and sensitive project back in 2010 and we occasionally bump into each other, usually at a run or local sportive and as we have a natter, I try not to stand too close if you know what I mean, Lycra is not flattering on a man of my age but Steve was built for sportswear. I was glad that Steve had already ran so did give me a chance to chat and lovely to get to know each other as we headed back into Warwick and at one point coming within sight of home, tempting but as the conversation flowed, I was happy to keep running. I liked the fact that although very focused and working to a plan, he does not take himself to seriously and has been known to run dressed as Dorothy to raise money for Dorothy House Hospice. A pleasure to run with Steve but no video today, not that he has ever mentioned it since (ok maybe one or twice) ....

The headline on Steve's Facebook page speaks volumes of the man.

"Live life today because no one knows what tomorrow brings"

The run with Steve was a massive confidence boost for me, which I needed, always appreciate straight talking people and our conversations during the run made me realise that the world is full of some amazing people and if I wanted to do good things, I needed to surround myself with great people like Steve.

Returning home, the events of recent weeks, with the terror attack at the Ariana Grande concert in May at Manchester Arena killing 22 people and injuring 100's more and during the previous week, the tragic Grenfell Tower fire taking another 72 life's and with many others losing everything brought home the fragility of life but more so, the amazing people who step up to the plate in times of need. The stories of ordinary people, if there is such a thing, just getting on with whatever was needed had an impact on myself as well as many others. This was clear in the content of my blog.

17th June 2017 - Helping Hands

I am only a few weeks into the crazy year but already the challenge is changing me and my perception of life. The recent events in London and Manchester just highlight that the world is full of some amazing people; you only need to watch the media and hear the stories of people helping people. Dropping everything to help others, giving of time, belongings and money to people that just happened to be in the wrong place at the wrong time and theirs lives have changed for ever and for some ended. These people are not talking about the problems, debating the issues and the next steps but getting out there and actually doing something about the problem to make a difference.

Running with fifty six different people during the year was always going to be one of my favourite challenges but with having ran with three people already in the last couple of weeks, this particular challenge is opening a whole new world and thoughts. The conversation just flows and so interesting to hear peoples take on life and just the best way to have a chat surpassed only by over a pint maybe. The journal was a great idea and loving reading the comments post run. So if you get a tap on the shoulder, be prepared – you will be a captive audience but does work both ways. The word of the day, from today's run with Steve – awesome!

I am hoping to get out some with a couple of special people and looking forward to hearing and sharing their stories with you – that will truly be awesome!

Thanks again for all your support and stay safe.

CITY #2 – MAHON

Another favourite of mine and not to dissimilar to Gothenburg, a bustling harbour and charismatic city. Being in Menorca at the start of the summer and the arrival of warmer temperatures, the best time to run is early doors before the sun turns up the heat. My run took me along the waterside path and a cooling sea breeze before heading up into the heart of the city and to the empty streets just showing signs of waking up to start a new day. Normally Placa de Colon is a busy square with restaurants and shops on every side, the statue of a little girl overshadowed by the hustle and bustle, but at this time of the morning whist most folks are in bed, the beautiful enchanting La Niña bathed in the ethereal dawn light seems to almost come to life and watches the early risers going about the business of their day. Two cities done and already the challenge was getting under my skin. Even the simplest of challenges on the surface, looking like just a bit of fun already were far more than that. I could have rolled over and had another hour in bed but I would not have seen the city waking up ready to start a new day, the slate wiped clean and the promise of a fresh start. Life is like that where ever you are.

"Sunrise - Sunset"

Thank you to Sheldon Harnick, lyric from the classic musical Fiddler on the Roof and very fitting. Today was going to be a long one - the challenge to see the Sunrise and Sunset on the same day.

I thought seeing the sunrise and set on the same day would be one of the easier challenges of the year but was surprisingly a lot trickier that I would have imagined. It was all about the logistics, timing and most of all location. Sun rises in the East and sets in the West, I learnt that much at school and I had conveniently arranged to be on holiday in Menorca for the next challenge so the chance of seeing the sun at both ends of the day was achievable and hopefully very enjoyable. The summer brings better weather and hopefully clearer skies but the down side is short nights and I wanted to the sun make its entrance on the longest day so that was going to require an early wakeup call but no one said it was going to be easy. I love the mornings and with the promise of a stunning sunrise was going to be worth the early exit from my bed. The mornings are my favourite time of the day and I am a regular dawn runner even at home and even in the middle of winter, I might have mentioned that once or twice before. Today was warm even at this time of day, I had done my research and ran around the bay to get the clear view of the sun emerging from the sea. The prize was worth the effort, to say it was breath-taking does not even get close to a suitable word to describe the stunning arrival of a new day. I had my words ready and strategically arranged the camera to capture the sunrise and my face. To be honest, I didn't need to say anything. Nature had successfully provided the image and the narration and did not really need the human intervention as perfection could not be improved. Moved to tears, I gave myself the time to enjoy this experience and as I stood and pondered, I thought of my parents, my family and those close to me, I reflected on my life and how lucky I was. I was able to enjoy every day and plan the future. For those living on the streets, neither are a given. I ran back to the apartment, grateful for my life. Seeing the same sun depart later in the day would be a little easier and for that, I would have company. On the cliff top above the deep blue sea, I stood in silence with the woman I love, as with the sunrise, the beautiful end of the day needed no words. The perfect end to another day in paradise.

Four challenges complete in as many weeks, 3 runners and two cities, not bad for the first month.

Get it down ya son!

To give me a fighting chance of surviving the year and I need to have a few challenges that could be over and done with little preparation. I like my food and not really a fussy eater but challenge number five to many people would be part of a daily health routine but for me the idea of eating a raw egg was not one I was looking forward to. Rather than just "doing it" I took advantage of an invitation from Mark and Jane Bates from the Sunday running group for coffee at theirs after our run and used the garden gathering as backdrop to the task and provide some added theatre along with a chance to rattle the bucket. With Libby, my eldest daughter and keen runner on hand to provide photographic evidence and moral support, I opted to have my coffee and bacon butties after the challenge just in case the egg wanted to make a guest appearance not wanting to remain in my tummy.

With the stage set, finding a sunlit corner of the patio and in chucking distance of the flower border if the challenge did not go to plan and vomiting resulted, I said a few words, some thank you's before commencing a count down, "five, four ......".

It was more about texture rather than taste, to be honest, it tasted like an omelette but the texture, that was not to my liking. Rather like the runners in the Two Castles, the egg stayed on mass as it slithered down my throat and thankfully staying put. A round of applause brought the challenge to an end, short and sweet but way outside of comfort zone. I don't think I will be adding a raw egg to my morning routine any day soon. Now where's that coffee?

RUN #4 – ANNE OLEXA

It was almost as if it was planned, but was pure fluke. To run on the Fourth of July with runner #4 was a sheer coincidence, but to run with my great friend from Detroit on American Independence Day was not, it had to be done really. Anne had a surprise for me, she had kindly bought us some great matching T shirts for the occasion with a profound statement "Make America Great Britain again" on a funky Anglo-American backdrop. We looked every bit a team and Anne would become to play a big part of the challenge year. I have known Anne for over 14 years, meeting through our daughters' school and soon becoming one of my closest friends and ironically, we lived in the same neighbourhood in Detroit back in the eighties and never knew it. She was a girl from the mid-west, I was a stranger in strange land, funny the way life plays out. Although I run with Anne a lot with our weekly dawn rendezvous more like therapy than exercise, todays outing was no less special. We chatted, we laughed and on a lovely evening to run, a very different way to celebrate the Fourth of July along with the debut of the post run video. Only a few weeks into the year, we did not know but this would not be the last time Anne would be by my side as I took on a challenge. I already liked that the challenge had almost taken on its own personality and had become much more than just an idea. Anne and I had shared many great adventures over the years and is always in the thick of the good stuff of life, but would the challenges ahead take Anne out of her comfort zone? You are going to wait a good few pages more to find out. Tonight, was very special and even Anne's dog Sadie was keen to get in on the action and in the post run photographs.

Run #5 – Lianne Kirkman

This took a bit of doing, I had only known Lianne for a few months so I thought a run together would be a good way to get to know each other better. I wanted to meet the real person and find out what makes the driving force behind Helping Hands get out of bed in the morning and take on the world, making such a difference to many people in my hometown. She would not mind me saying that, Lianne is not a fan of running so she did take a bit of persuading to put on the trainers and join me for a trot around Victoria Park in Leamington. A common misconception when I asked for people to run with that it would all be about running, all sporty and competitive but this is absolutely not the case, I just wanted to get out and spread the word. A natural people person and a whizz on social media, we were soon "live" on Facebook. Once we had done PR stuff, we chatted, and hearing Lianne's story moved me to tears. I often wonder what makes people who they are, fate, timing, right place - right time, it's all a matter of your own thoughts. I do find that life does throw some surprises and connections spring out of nowhere. Running with Lianne, we talked about a variety of subjects and interesting to find out we had similar views on faith and is all about being the best person you can be although I for one do not always get it right. I loved running with Lianne and felt like I had got to know the person behind the public face of Helping Hands and I was delighted that she was happy for me to share her story. This would feature in a one of my weekly blogs in the weeks to come and decided to let Lianne tell her story in her own words.

DARE TO BE DIFFERENT

Talk about seizing the moment, I have never had my face painted not even as a child. (I was a funny kid - trust me on that) I may have occasional tried to emulate Fish from Marillion once or twice in my youth but I am talking about full on face paint like "Young Kenny" for all you Phoenix Nights fans out there. If I was going to get my face painted, I didn't want a butterfly on my cheek, oh no, I wanted to look like a tiger. I had come to the annual Guide Dogs summer fair to see if I could arrange a guide to take me for a run but although I made contact and had the bones of an idea, unfortunately the plan did not come to any but the visit to the Leamington base did give me the perfect opportunity and the chance to join the queue albeit all children and fulfil a lifelong ambition and to be transformed into a tiger. Quickly explaining to those around me and in ear shot of the painters that I hadn't lost the plot or just been thrown out of the beer tent and that this was part of a year of challenges and some more PR but the looks on the children's faces, generally an open book, told me that they were not buying my explanation and that in fact I was mad and I might have had an alcoholic beverage, neither true although I enjoyed the chance to sit still for five minutes during what was turning out to be a busy day already. With Julie on hand recording the inner tiger in me taking shape, I realised that I might just have to spend the day like this. We were off to a family BBQ later in the day so a drive to Coventry and a chance to show off my new image. What would the grandchildren think?

I paid my money and with a number of well wishes from the still bemused gathering I headed off to see if I could get another couple of challenges arranged whilst I had the eye of the tiger.

Something involving heights was on the list and opposite the face painter was a nice shiny fire engine which could only mean one thing, firemen! I had already opened discussions with Tim, a fireman friend before the year started, I liked the idea of a trip on Simon snorkel or a turntable ladder and get a birds eye view of my home town. I think that would challenge my fear of heights. I chatted and name dropped and to my surprise they had heard of me and happily gave me the top man's name and the approach I could take with the boss. Following the advice, I sent in my letter and unfortunately that was the last I heard from my fireman friends. Not every egg would be a bird, I knew that from life and before the 56 challenges were completed, I would hit dead ends on many occasions. No one said it was going to be easy.

As for the rest of the day as a tiger, this was one of many times that looking different and standing out from the crowd was not always that comfortable. As for the grandchildren, they did not bat an eyelid! I guess that's what comes of having Grandpa Steve as your grandad.

9th July 2017- Faith, Hope and Charity

And so the journey continues … unfortunately life did get in the way a little this week as it has a happy knack of doing. I did get the chance to run with two great people in my quest to run with 56 different people through the year and it is lovely to hear from people wanting to come run with me, some old friends, along with strangers I have yet to know, although Daniel Craig continues to be a little elusive.

To run with Lianne Kirkman was fabulous and to hear her story was an inspiration and gave me a real boost to do the challenges and for the year ahead. We talked of our faith and interestingly we have similar values, it's about the doing rather that the talking. She is a real legend and that goes for the Helping Hands team as a whole.

I did have an offer for someone to come and run with me, this lady is not a runner but wants to get involved, to quote her "I have seen helping hands on Facebook loads and donated a couple of bits before, I had an experience today with a homeless man and feel so blessed to have what I have which isn't loads but I have a home and a lovely family and I feel I want to help the charity, maybe a fundraising run? I literally have never run before though…..."

She went on to suggest that she is tempted to do a half marathon or something. Go Girl!!

I am looking forward to meeting up with her and help with her challenge; I continue to be really moved by the people I am meeting.

As the sun continues to shine, the challenges continue into a new month, I thought I would give you an update of the "scores on the doors"

Challenges completed – 6 (50 remaining)

Challenges started – 2 - both about 10% complete

Money raised £503 with another £70 to go on for the Zero to Hero coffee morning/egg challenge

Thank you everyone for your help and support, really appreciated

Run #6 – Tracey Murphy

I had to run with Tracey or RB (Running Buddy as I always call her), having been one of my faithful dawn runners for many years when I lived in Lillington we are never short of something to talk about and a nurse too which is always bonus. When Tracey took on the responsibility of two dogs who would often join us on our early morning outings and away took us away from the busy streets around Lillington and into the quieter fields around Stoneleigh but today Chester and Busby stayed at home. Even though we have ran in and around north Leamington for years, Tracey wanted to include a local landmark that would fall victim to HS2, the Cubbington Pear tree. Having stood guard over the rolling countryside of Warwickshire for over 250 years it would soon make way for progress. One of the country's oldest and largest wild pear trees was chosen by the public as England's Tree of the Year for 2015. Sad to see this tree and the stunning countryside around it replaced by a swath of concrete and steel so travellers can arrive 10 minutes quicker. Will I see the high speed rail link finished in my life time, maybe but seems to be a lot of talking at the moment. Mother of four, a run is a great opportunity to catch up on the gossip and to hear what the family are up too. I miss our morning runs since moving to Warwick and life got in the way so a run with Tracey was a must and on my list from day one. Also on my list, was fellow Strider, Richard Bicknell who had made me welcome since my first run with Leamington based athletes club. Unfortunately, Richard and I's run was not to be having died suddenly on Wednesday 10th May 2017 just before my challenge year started, doing what he loved, running with others. So it was fitting that we talked fondly of him as we ran and felt that in some small way, he had been involved.

This run is dedicated for you my friend.

RIP Richard Bicknell 3rd March 1962 - 10th May 2017

Run #7 Steve Mason City #3 - Coventry

With so many tasks to complete, on occasion I would have the opportunity to combine challenges on the list to get "two bangs for the buck" as the saying goes and today was one such day and a very special combination it was too. Coventry is on my door step and although I have spent a lot of time in and around the city over the years, I rarely had the chance to get into its soul. Dependant on your age, your thoughts of Coventry will be different. It might be the blitz, Two Tone or the infamous ring road, the city is poles apart from where I was born and grew up. It's a typical city with all the trappings that go with it, the Specials immortalised Coventry with their depressing view of the place in the 1981 hit single "ghost town" and the later the hard-hitting band The Enemy, giving a similar perspective of their home town in 2006 with their number 1 debut album "We live and die in these towns". Neither a good advertisement for the city so close to where I was born and my wife's hometown.

I found the early morning run with my good friend Steve Mason very poignant and thought provoking as we ran from the memorial park, through the leafy suburbs of Earlsdon over the infamous ring road and into the heart of the city. Still rubbing its sleepy eyes and not quite awake, the empty streets showing signs of another inner city Friday night with the occasion "pavement pizza" punctuating the route and marking the place where food and alcohol lost the battle to reside in a revellers stomach. As Steve and I headed through the back waters of this eclectic city, with old and new architecture, living side by side, with some doorways providing a home to many of the cities rough sleepers, the need to do something if was ever in doubt was reinforced. Although still early in the scheme of things, the dawn had pretty much turned into day as we ran into the ruins of Coventry cathedral. A graphic symbol of man's aggression on man alongside the new modern church that reinforced the message of hope and recovery. We stood in silence and looked in awe at the stunning stained-glass window that marked the entrance to the new cathedral. Our reflection insignificant in the impressive masterpiece, a moving but uplifting experience. Steve and I both lead busy lives and this chance to just take a few minutes out and just "be" was priceless and provided yet another lasting memory and a great photo too. As we ran, the conversation also provided a great quote which I used in my blog later the same day as we discussed the many reasons why people end up on the streets, "it's not about drugs and dropouts is it Steve? Very true, I hadn't realised how many ex-servicemen end up homeless after serving for queen and country, with the change from a structured, almost institutionalised life style to being plunged into the big wide world, many with the battle scars both physical and mentally of fighting the worlds battles on foreign shores too much to take. For some, slipping through the gaps in the system and ending up in the door way of an inner city department store, not sure that was ever in the plan as they dodged bullets in places with unpronounceable names in countries that joe public know nothing about except for the headlines on the evening news. Universities also provide a good proportion of the homeless, not dissimilar to the end of a tour in Afghanistan, ending a structured life to one without routine. A tough transition for many people to make and one without a robust solution that can only get worse as the institutional sausage machines churn out more and more potential customers for the streets of our towns and cities any the numerous charities and voluntary organisations that are there to help pick up the pieces.

A very though provoking run for sure and to change the mood completely, on returning to Kenilworth, we took Steve's' new running outfit, Herman the German that he planned to complete the Great North Run later in the year for a test run, the looks we got! In all a perfect start to the day.

15th July 2017 - Drugs and drop outs

The more I talk to people, the more the dialogue comes back to a recurring theme. Life can change in a moment, throwing us a curve ball. There is a misconception that most people on the streets or needing help are all in that situation as a result of alcohol or substance abuse, but these make up the minority, most are as a result of a change of circumstances. A relationship break up, the loss of a parent and I was amazed to hear that those leaving the Armed Forces often find it difficult to adjust and end up also needing help. The reasons are many, but for all, getting back to a stable and safe environment along with the ability to plan for a future, returns structure and self-esteem, turning heart ache and anxiety to smiles and I know not every egg's a bird as they say but seeing the stories of people helped by the two charities we together are helping, is heart-warming.

The knowledge that I am gathering from the experts that I am coming in contact with is becoming invaluable and it is lovely to share the learning with you.

Thank you for sharing the journey.

THE SOUP KITCHEN

The challenge was to help out at a soup kitchen but was so much more than ticking another one off the list. I was keen to get to the "coal face" as soon as possible and see the work Helping Hands were doing and start to understand the issues in my hometown, a shift at the nightly soup kitchen was a good start point. I ready did not know what to expect. Driving down to "the lighthouse", Helping Hands base in Leamington Spa, the air of uncertainty was apparent from both Julie and I with this being my first real exposure to the issues facing people out on the street. I was a little apprehensive to be honest, I have led a pretty sheltered or rather shielded life style. Always had a roof over my head and food to eat and although not wealthy by any stretch of the imagination, myself or my family have never gone without.

Arriving at the front of "the lighthouse", a delivery from one of Helping Hands local supporters was just being unloaded from the back of a van by a friendly gentleman from the Gurdwara Sahid, local Sikh temple, vegetable curry and rice and it smelt amazing. Having only been out of the car a matter of seconds, I was already touch by the kindness and generosity of my fellow man.

The soup kitchen didn't open for business until 6.30pm so gave Julie and I chance to meet some of the other volunteers and have a coffee along with getting our roles for the evening plus a few tips. I was already in awe of the regulars who were helping week in week out. We appreciated being in the company of old hands who soon had us feeling very much at home and part of the family. I was given a job, "keep the sugar bowl topped up Steve", I heard that request so many times as the night progressed and the nights customers arrived. I didn't get it, but after a few requests and a clear look of confusion on my face, I was taken to one side and let into the secret. Methadone, I was told, a drug used to help folks get off heroin and other narcotic drugs had the side effect of giving users a massive sugar craving so any drinks had a good addition of sugar. Doing some research regarding the other more intense side effects of methadone were not pleasant and can see why the road to rehabilitation can be a tough one.

I would like to say I arrived with an open mind but in my head, I had a preconception of the people that would turn up and how they would be, but I was wrong and I blame my sheltered upbringing and the media. I was overwhelmed and humbled, these folks were just normal people who life had dealt them a duff hand. As I mingled, I chatted, making sure everyone was fed and watered. A regular volunteer Sue invited me to go with her to hand out some food and drinks to those who, for a myriad of reasons, didn't want to come to the soup kitchen. I declined this time, I wasn't ready to be honest, tonight was a shock to my system and I needed to acclimatise a little. Julie just got with it, she does that so well, but I have to come around a little, but with the help of some amazing people, it didn't take long. I felt at ease and was keen do my bit and not just filling the sugar bowl. Respect is a two-way process and I was keen not to judge, it was a level playing field as far as I was concerned, I was taken aback by the politeness from many of tonight's customers, and without question I reciprocated. I was pulled up when I called someone mate, I have a name I was reminded - a good lesson.

One of the first people I met was Richard who I took an instant like to and out paths would cross many times in the challenge year and for a long time after.

Once tonight's customers headed back into the night, Julie and I took time to chat with Lianne and tonight's volunteer leader Jo Aston and reflect on the night. The emotion, which up to now, I had held inside, surfaced and it was clear the evening had got under my skin - I was inspired and motivated, not that I needed any more reasons to take on this crazy idea, Helping Hands was a good choice.

The atmosphere in the Lighthouse was warm, more like a big family meal rather than just a refuelling exercise for most of the customers or clients as the team always referred to the visitors as. Most were polite and loving the chance of company and a safe place for a chat as much as the food. Nothing went to waste and with the generosity of local shops and organisations, everyone left with full tummies and a something to eat away from the Lighthouse. Like all gatherings, the soup kitchen had rules, most based on courtesy and respect for others. I liked that and a good life lesson for all of us.

Inspired by the visit to the Lighthouse along with the opportunity to read Lianne's story which I had heard on our run earlier in the month, she agreed for me to share it with the world in my weekly blog making it a bit of an epic.....

22nd July 2017 - Lianne's story

As part of the 56notout journey, the intention was always to visit the coal face and see for myself some of the issues in our towns along with the work done by the local charity Helping Hands. Monday night is curry night at the drop in centre or soup kitchen as it's sometimes called. When Julie and I arrived to start our evening shift, the first impression was one of hope and generosity. The arrival of the curry from the local Sikh temple along with the cakes and pasties left over from the days sales at Greggs brought me to tears. Not because of my love of curry and pastry but the seeing people helping others and sense of community. It was a busy session and to meet some of the local characters was a life changing experience and to see where the money goes was a real boost to the challenge. We met some amazing and lovely people on both sides of the "counter" and we are gaining more awareness of life on the streets with more learning to come I am sure.

The need is now and it's not all about the money, help and support can come in many different forms and charities like Helping Hands are always ready to take you up on any help you can give.

One of the 56 challenges is to run with 56 different people which is giving me a great opportunity to run with old friends and new people alike and to hear their story and spread the word.

Recently I ran with Lianne Kirkman, founder of Helping Hands. We talked of life and its meanings and I was touch by her open and honesty about her own life.

This is Lianne's story in her own words….

My reason for running Helping Hands is a very personal one and like several of our current volunteers and people we support, we all have a story and at some point in our lives have needed a Helping Hand...

Four years ago my husband Paddy and I were in a desperate state where we were both crying out for help. Due to a stressful situation at work I began to suffer from depression and it only seemed to be getting worse by me being there so I decided to quit my job. However, the timing was far from perfect as we were in the middle of a building project at home and by not having my extra wage coming in and still having all the regular bills to pay, it meant we spiralled quickly into a debt worth thousands of pounds.

This only made my depression worse. I got to a point where I struggled to get out of bed most days and I couldn't even face leaving the house, so Paddy had to literally hold the family together, taking the kids to and from school, cooking all the meals and doing all the housework, which inevitably put a huge strain on him and our relationship.

I was desperately ill and really struggled with the guilt of knowing that my depression and the situation we were in was making life unbearable for the family. One evening I felt completely broken and I could no longer cope with my depression and how it was affecting everyone, so I decided to leave home believing the lie that everyone's lives would be much better without me. I went to the Leamington train station contemplating which train would take me the furthest away, so that no one could ever find me or which train I should jump in front of to end it all... I remember looking at the sky and really crying out to ask if God was there and if he was, then why did he not appear remotely interested in helping me and our family!

Crazily Paddy located me on his "find my iPhone" app which my phone was still connected to and on silent in my bag. He sent one of his friends to the station to find me and to encourage me to go home. He came to tell me Paddy and my kids were all at home crying waiting and begging for mummy to come home.

Thankfully the thoughts of my two beautiful children being so upset were what stopped me acting on those destructive thoughts that night and I ended up back at home. Still hurting and still unsure how things could ever get any better.

A few weeks later we met up with an amazing couple Steph and Geoff Devlin who ran the homeless soup kitchen in Leamington for 24 years through their project Leamington Christian Mission. As well as the homeless soup kitchen, Leamington Christian Mission helped families in poverty in the area by providing food, clothing and furniture in times of need. Their motto was simply 'meeting the need'.

Steph & Geoff Devlin proved to be an answer to that prayer I had said at the station a few weeks before because they came alongside us, encouraged us & gave us food parcels, toiletries and clothes for our kids among other things that we would normally spend our money on each month. This meant the money we had coming in from Paddy's wage could all now be used to help us claw out of our debt.

What also helped was Steph & Geoff encouraged me to volunteer for their project to help me have a focus & target to get me out of bed each week. (This is why we now actively encourage volunteering in Helping Hands for those going through difficult situations). I started working in their warehouse sorting through donations once a week and eventually Steph asked me &Paddy to join their evening outreach team at their homeless soup kitchen. I had worked previously as a drug and alcohol nurse in a rehab in wales, volunteered with various homeless projects in Birmingham, Leeds and Scunthorpe, I had helped set up an outreach project and a drop-in for street girls in Coventry and started a number of community projects within a local church (and funnily enough had called those projects Helping Hands), so working with the homeless and people with additional needs was right up my street and something I have always had a passion for. My time volunteering proved so valuable in helping me regain my confidence, self-belief & self-esteem. It also helped relight the vision in me to work with people struggling with life controlling issues such as homelessness, depression & people with addictions.

Being surrounded by positive people at the Leamington Christian Mission who genuinely cared for me & Paddy and the kids was just what we had been craving. They provided the friendships we were desperate for during our most difficult time of need.

Eventually and after several months of volunteering at the Leamington Christian Mission and after having other people come alongside to support us (Heather at Warwick Gates counselling - Ann Hibbert and the team at The Well and a few faithful friend's), I was thinking and feeling much more positive about life and about our future and I decided I was ready go back to paid work to continue with my nursing career. I got a part time job at a local GP surgery and this helped us pay back more of the remaining debt we were now gradually reducing, but I still continued to volunteer for the soup kitchen in an evening and once a week in their warehouse.

In December 2014, Steph and Geoff made the decision to retire after they lost their storage warehouse to a building contract and they decided to give many of the items in storage to a lady who had begun a small project helping local people in Kenilworth which was also called Helping Hands. This Helping Hands started in December 2013 with one lady wanting to help a homeless man she had seen on the streets. She asked friends and family on her Facebook page to donate items she could take to a homeless shelter in Coventry and she had a huge response, so gave so many items to the shelter and the rest was distributed to local families in need.

When Steph and Geoff Devlin finally retired and much of their items handed over to the Kenilworth Helping Hands, I asked the lady who was running this amazing small community outreach if I could get involved and help out as a volunteer. She went on to say her husband had recently found work in America and she was looking for someone to take on what she had started, to take it to the next level by developing it further. She felt after meeting with me a couple more times that I was the right person to take this on... so after several conversations with my husband, Steph Devlin and other volunteers I had worked with in the Leamington Christian Mission, I decided to go for it. I now felt so ready for the challenge and wanted so much more to help people who were also going through difficult times.

We created a trustee board in March 2015 and registered with the Charity Commission to create the charity "Helping Hands Community Project".

It has grown so quickly in the last two and a half years since registering and we have been completely overwhelmed by the generosity of the local communities of Leamington, Warwick and Kenilworth who have completely embraced the charity and so many people, organisations and businesses have got involved in some way. We now have an amazing family of 60+ volunteers and 4 paid staff.

I believe peoples willingness to be a part of Helping Hands is partly because everyone can relate at some point to needing a Helping Hand. It is undoubtedly also due to the fact that the local homeless situation in our towns has seemed to increase and become more visible and people are really wanting to know how to help. Helping Hands among other local homeless projects give local people the opportunity to be involved in meeting the needs of local people by giving of their time, skills/gifts, money or things that will get distributed and given directly to those who need it most, the most vulnerable in our towns.

Two and a half years have passed since registering and we are now based in Leamington Spa, but still cover Kenilworth and Warwick and surrounding areas. We still distribute items to local individuals and families in need in the area through our house2home project. We give out donated household goods, furniture, clothing, and toiletries etc., all of which were given to us when we were struggling as a family and in our own place of need.

We now run the Leamington soup kitchen to homeless and vulnerable adults 3 nights a week and a breakfast drop-in on a Tuesday morning. We have a charity shop and we are also about to open a cafe. We offer day time support through work experience, training and offer qualifications in NVQ customer service, retail, warehouse, maths and computers (in partnership with national charity CRISIS) and we are soon to offer hospitality, catering & food hygiene courses, all of which are geared to helping people regain their confidence, self-esteem and self-belief to get back on their feet and hopefully back in to work.

Our vision is a big one and we hope to open more shops and eventually have our own place for vulnerable women that they can call home and offer a place of refuge and restoration.

Our own personal journey of needing a helping hand is the motivation behind us being involved in this charity and many of our volunteers all have their own personal stories for being involved. We are so thankful that we as a family were able to claw our way out of our difficulties, but it was only made possible by people reaching out, rebuilding our confidence & being a helping hand. If we hadn't had that support, I'm not sure where or how things would have turned out.

Ill health (physical or mental), a death in the family, family breakdown, debts, unemployment etc. are all common causes of homelessness in the UK so Helping Hands is a community project ran by local people, for local people to help prevent homelessness and to help people in their time of need to move on from their difficult circumstances.

And together as a community we are definitely making a difference to so many people's lives.

RUN #8 – BETHAN GWYNN

Today was a chance to run at my favourite time of the day, dawn. I love to get up and get out before the workday starts, the weather was kind today. Although I have known Bethan for many years when I was a member of Spa Striders, a local running club based in Royal Leamington Spa, hence the club names nod to the famous water. Bethan is still a member, but I left the club to start my own group which better suited my ability and philosophy to running. Today was the first time that we had ran together, just the two of us and was lovely to get to know each other without the pressure of keeping up with pack. Bethan is a really good runner but still has the passion for just getting the trainers on and enjoying being out in the fresh air. Combining her passion for running and the idea of helping others understanding the issues facing runners, Bethan invested time and effort to become a qualified physiotherapist, little did I know that I would be need those skills before the challenge year was over but that's for another chapter.

We headed out into the countryside, skirting one of the area's biggest housing estates, Woodloes Park, although you would not know as we ran along Woodloes Lane, the established hedgerow shielding us from the houses where no doubt the occupants were stirring from a nights slumber ready for another day on the hamster wheel. We headed out into the tranquillity of open farmland, a stone's throw from life but as we ran along the well-trodden paths through the fields and along the edge of the Warwickshire a Golf course before head back to Guys Cliffe and past the beautiful Saxon Mill and across the bridge over the river Avon. Staying on the banks of the river in the shadow of the ruins of Guys Cliffe

Manor, so much history and hiding secrets of a chequered past. A favourite place to run of mine and turned out to be Bethan's too, we are lucky to have so many places to run on our door step. Another stunning start to the day.

Run #9 – Tim Stooks

A blast from the past or it's a small world. Similar to Bethan,
 Tim was a Spa Strider too and another person who I have
known a while but never ran with. Tim only lives a few
streets away so I having loitered on his door step, we headed
off for a run and a chat. We had only gone a short distance
when we realised we had a mutual friend and a real blast from
the past. I hadn't heard the name Dave Cooling for a good
few years having worked together back in the nineties at
RDS, in Southam. The memories came flooding back and
Dave would be a great person to run with but with enough
on my plate at the moment, I left the task of getting out for a
beer with Dave as a challenge for Tim to make happen.
Running on home ground, the chat was very much sport
based and clearly Tim had a very different approach to the
sport than I have but good to get the trainers on.

RUN #10 – TAWANDA BWERUDZA

I work in the same office as Tawanda, we chat in the kitchen over a coffee but that's pretty much the extent of our daily contact, so I was delighted when he agreed to run with me. This guy looked fit so I might just have my work cut out to keep up with him, time would tell. We decided to run after work, based on the edge of Birmingham Airport, you would think that running options would be limited but if you look hard enough, you can find hidden gems of sanctuary. Tawanda, born in Harare, came to England some 15 years ago leaving his native country of Zimbabwe with his mother as a result of a better job, was fascinating to run with. It was obvious that he had a rough idea of what I was doing but was intrigued to understand why. In my country Steve, Tawanda added, if my brother has nothing then we all have nothing. If my brother needs help, I help him. No need for charities looking after those who need help, the family look after family, friends look after friends. We don't have special homes for the elderly, the family take care of the older members of the family. I don't get it Steve. I had never thought that deep before but it's true. In many countries and cultures, the family is everything. Go to Spain and good luck finding an old people's home, just not the need, family is everything. I thoroughly enjoyed getting to know more about Tawanda and he of me. It always amazes me how quickly the knowledge sharing progress happens on a run. With every step, the better you know the person by your side and the world we live in. We definitely do not have all the answers to life's problems and clearly something to learn from others, I found the short run with this softly spoken gentleman gave me a different view of my own planet. I hadn't realised but on the streets of own towns and cities, you rarely see people other than white in need of help from passing strangers.... I'll leave that thought with you.

THE CIRCLE OF TRUST OR THE ART OF LETTING GO

I have already told you that some very early advice from Gary McKee was to hand over social media to someone less old should we say but letting go of the reins comes at a price. Whist sunning myself in Minorca and ticking off a couple of challenges, Emma was making me pay and frantically arranging a challenge that was never on the list but after the public vote, became challenge number 8.

Taking advantage of a Wi-Fi hotspot, you can imagine the look of horror on my face when I checked of this surprise post on social media.

!!!!SHARE SHARE SHARE!!!!

Emma here again and I've decided, since Mr 56 Not Out himself is away sunning himself on his holidays and can't protest, that this week I am going to boost the likes on the page and have LOADS of fun planning to torture him on his return.

Anyone who likes the 56 Not Out page, likes and shares this post and donates just £2 to the Just Giving page will be eligible to vote for one of the following to happen to Steve on his return:-

Vote 1 - Ice bucket challenge (the biggest bucket of iced water we can get tipped right over his head)

Vote 2 - Leg wax (I draw the line at back, sack and crack do we really want to see those photos!?)

Vote 3 - Karaoke - open to suggestions for songs too!

Vote 4 - Raw onion challenge - he has to eat the whole thing in one sitting!

Vote 5 - A good old fashioned gunging!

Please like, share and comment with the one you'd most like to see (either on this post or on the Just Giving page) Don't forget to donate! Enter as many times as you like. The one with the most votes wins - in the event of a tie we will put the two options in a hat and pick the winner.

We will post a video of the torture here on the 56 Not Out page and will give details on how to watch the live show on the day.

The Facebook page went crazy, with comments, pledges and shares going into overdrive, I could do nothing but watch as my fate was at the hands of the public.

Resistance is futile I soon learnt, and it soon became apparent that from the choice of the five options, having my body waxed was obviously becoming the clear winner and a chance to vote coming at a small fee, put some money in the pot too. I could do nothing but lie on my sun bed watch the fate of my bodily hair being decided by the growing band of followers. To say several work colleagues got behind this challenge was an understatement and I feared for my pubic hair on more than one occasion but once the news that this hair removing extravaganza was going to happen in public in Smith Street during Warwick folk festival, I knew of dignity would remain at least somewhat intact. Katie Barnes, from a local beauty salon, Simply Nails had already offered to wax me for nothing and with the flourish of media, both social and local press, whipped up by Emma. I knew that this was going to be a great challenge.

Keeping an eye on base camp using the wonders of technology provided one of the many funny images as the daunting FaceTime screen shot was blasted over social media. Topless showing sun burnt and soon to be no more bodily hair. Thanks Emma, that girl really does know how to play social media.

By the time we returned home, the local press had already confirmed that they would be send a photographer to capture the occasion I knew my pride was going out of the window along with my body hair with every passing minute.

I have never experienced waxing before and to date any hair removal was usually done using traditional methods with soap and a razor so hearing the abundant advice about what to do and what not to do to not too much for my blood pressure especially when I was told by a medical friend to take anti inflammatories and pain killers beforehand, bloody hell folks what have I signed up for!

But every day is a school day and bowing to the knowledge of others, I took a chemical cocktail of goodies that should cover all bases and on arriving at the salon in my swimming trunks and a t shirt, the glass of fizz was perfect addition to the potion. I couldn't feel a thing already, nothing to this waxing lark. The treatment couch and the great publicity posters gave the passing folkies, who for the record would have benefited much more than myself from some hair removal, and that was just the women, clues of my pending fate.

Team 56 were in attendance with t shirts and buckets to spread the message and extract a coin or two from the good folk of Warwick and visitors alike.

Noon was the chosen hour for the fun to start, plenty of people around by then and as history has shown, public torture does attract a crowd. Chatting to the mayor of Warwick sat in my swimming trucks in the middle of town was a strangely surreal experience but anyone who would listen to my story was fair game for me.

So the time arrived, and it was time to go hairless for the homeless as Eileen Kiddell, a work colleague, who I am sure was only there to see me suffer, aptly put it as another male and less cruel mate whispered "rather you than me mate" as Alex started to tear a strip of me I felt like I was in the colosseum being throw to the lions. Prodding the soles of my tender feet, Eileen reminded me, "the more you scream, the more they'll pay". The photographer arrived on cue and wanting the shot that captured the moment of pain and anticipation, I did not have to resort to any of my limited acting skills. I was nervous, and it did hurt but I was delighted to hear from Alex that I wasn't bleeding that much. That's ok then. Focusing on the reason I was lying half naked in the street kept me going but what was going to be having my legs waxed at the start of the discussions to legs, back and chest by the time the day arrived was enough for any man to take but in response to "Here's another twenty quid if you do his armpits", I had had enough. Julie sensed this as the banter stopped and I went quiet, I was fast retreating in to Steve's world and is not one of my favourite places to be honest, I only retreat here as a last resort but with the last of any hair gone it was time for a few photos and a very much deserved beer.

Within the space of an hour and watched by a staggering 4700 people on Facebook, I now had the body of a young boy all ready for my holiday the following week. I was looking forward to strutting my stuff on the beaches of Sicily, not sure my wife agreed.

Whatever the holiday photos looked like, the fund-raising pot got a much-needed boost and some great PR in the local press and even featured in one of Ken Wilkins, Leamington Courier cartoonist weekly master piece as he reflected on the story in the previous weeks paper.

RUN # 1 1 – RICHARD WARD

Little did we know what lay ahead, when I first met Richard back in 2004. We worked together at Jaguar but unaware that we both would soon be first time parents until when we rocked up at pre-natal classes ahead of the arrival of our respective first born children. Our faces showed our apprehension looking like rabbits in the headlights neither really prepared for imminent role of fatherhood. Mitchell was the first to arrive on the 7th December 1994, I had to wait a few weeks more until Olivia Rose Atherton to make her grand entrance into the world, choosing Christmas Day to make her appearance and making the front page of the Coventry Evening Telegraph. As we ran we talked of our kids and the journey they had travelled and pondered the world that we had brought them into. The pride We both felt for our offspring was clear and we recognised that we hadn't done a bad job after all.

We talked about life and our own journeys touching on the plight of the homeless. Richard reminded me that I once chose a car based on the fact I could live in it if things did not go well and the challenging period I found myself in didn't go to plan. Pretty tough to hear but true and a poignant reminder of the fragility of life. Fortunately I didn't need to live in my car and the stormy seas of my life did calm. Away from parenthood and work, Richard and I paths often cross with many mutual friends, usually at running events, Richard is usually home and showered as I reach the half way point but he is built like a runner. Another thought provoking run and nice to have a coffee and catch up with Richard's wife, Andrea too.

Where have the years gone?

Run #12 – Fiona/Sue/Seaforth/ Margaret aka Kersley Running Club

I liked todays run, special in many ways. A new place to run and someone new. In fact actually ran with four people but only counted it as one off my of 56 challenge. Today's new runners came courtesy of Emma who continued to promote the 56notout challenge, this time to her work colleagues. Meeting at Fiona's house with the promise of more people joining in the fun. I had exchanged messages with her and what was going to be just the two of us, developed into something different and the promise of cake! I loved running with this eclectic mix of people and some real hidden talent. I learnt about Seaforths baby, the Kersley Running Club. I loved his passion, my absolute favourite word of mine, this group ran with passion. 'Passion' is the word, when the day comes for me to leave the mother ship, I would like that word to appear in my eulogy, although I can think of many other words that might make a guest appearance. Stubborn, annoying, impatient are a few but I am not in any hurry to find out for real. Marmite as my wife calls me, not sure what that means but she does remind me that I'm an acquired taste, good job she likes marmite. We talked as we ran, and as I have mentioned already, you do get to know each other with every step. Seaforth had his hands firmly on the reins, I liked that and he made sure everyone did the best they could, "no maybe tomorrow" with this group. After more laps of Bedworth Park than I was hoping for, he led the group back to Fiona's house and of course cake. I like this group, lovely people and they have cake, I promised to return.

30th July 2017 - Life is not a rehearsal

I have heard this phrase a few times this week, you only get one shot at this so need to make the most of it. Work/life balance always seems to come up in conversation a lot too especially on the 1 on 1 runs that are making up one of the 56 challenges and to be honest is the one I am enjoying most so far. What is not to like, running with amazing people in some beautiful places and a captive audience but that does work both ways. Listening to people's view of the world and what makes them tick is a real pleasure and giving me the drive and motivation to continue. I can already see the early signs of ideas in people's faces that maybe a change in direction or a tweak to a routine might lead to a life changing decision, please don't blame me but if you don't know where you are going, any road will take you there.

Taking time to make time is pretty important, time with friends and family is everything. You may have already seen or heard the well aired story of the empty jar? There is your homework, check out YouTube – empty jar life lesson.........

Two months into this year of challenges, what I have learnt?

People are amazing, I heard a phrase just before I was about to head off on this crazing journey," if you want to do good things, surround yourself with great people", so true.

You only need to ask, but be clear what you want, still not so good at that one but I am learning.

Watch who you leave in charge of social media and I actual liked my body hair – these lessons are linked! (Thanks Emma – you are doing a top job !) I liked the phrase "hairless for the homeless"

Scores on the doors

Challenges completed – 8 (48 remaining)

Challenges started – 3 with another 12 or so in the diary.

Money raised £793

Thank you to everyone who is following, helping, donating and, and, and – really appreciated.

Enjoy the summer and go pick some black berries!!

As July turned into August, the focus of our attention changed and the 56notout challenge had to take a back seat as we were reminded of the harsh realities of life. We get a life lesson every time we board an aeroplane and listen to the flight attendants safety briefing- "in the event of the loss of cabin pressure, please put on your own mask before helping others". For the next few weeks my wife and our family took priority as we prepared for the last few days of my father-in-law's long and full life.

Not sure of the reason but I did drop into the lighthouse, the Leamington base of Helping Hands and had a chat with Lianne and out of the blue, I struck up a conversation with one of the shops regularly visitors. The impromptu dialogue really touched me and yet again, got under my skin. I have been fortunate, I guess, more luck than judgement and although life has not been easy, I have always had a roof over my head and to talk to some who had not had it so easy was tough to take in. Lianne, subtlety slide away and let the lady open up to me. I admired her straight talking and honesty, she didn't know me from Adam but clearly she knew I was not there to judge. Her words spelling out the lifecycle of the journey of many. Hard hitting stuff and my blog summed up my emotions and by the time I published it, Ron had threw the towel in and at the amazing age of 95 he called it a day, passing away peacefully, a true gentleman to the end.

5th August 2017 - Borrow, steal, beg

A tough week in camp 56notout and we appreciate your kind thoughts.

The challenge took a back seat but I did manage to catch up with Lianne at the Lighthouse. A spontaneous chat with some amazing people gave some real food for thought. Asking someone who has hit the bottom and is now on the way up what is actually needed was a real education. She spoke of the downward spiral that some people experience, she said that there are three phases, first you borrow, then you steal, then you beg - sobering stuff. I want to go back and carry on the conversation in more depth but it was clear that although a meal, a hot drink and some clean clothes was a great help, these people need a future and a clear path off the streets, the lady spoke of the triangle. A roof, a job and a life and to have something to aim for is the hope and for someone to believe that their life is worth living. Those on the streets need more than a meal and being sent on their way, returning the next day to repeat the process, the circle needs to be broken. The conversations will continue for sure on future visits to the Lighthouse, together, the journey will progress and build. Thank you for sharing this journey with me.

This week's blog is dedicated to Ron Pickering, a true legend and a gentleman 1922 - 2017

TIME TO REFLECT

When I embarked on the challenge year, I was oblivious to that fact that maybe not everyone in my immediate family would not see the project's completion. Born in 1922, Ron Pickering aka G, Julie's father was one of life's gentleman. At 95 years old, Ron certainly lived a full life, but he told me many times that he didn't want to live to a hundred. Always a man ahead of his time, as Julie always fondly described him, I wasn't really sure what he thought of the challenge idea. Generous to many charities, he had his favourites that he religiously supported, and I always hoped that he approved of what I was doing.

The last few months have been a challenge in itself, juggling hospital visits, relocation and towards the end progressively more emotional visits to a local care home. With his dwindling thirst for technology, a sure sign that his time on this planet was coming to an end, the short visits became more about closure and finishing the final chapter in the book of life. Although inevitable and predictable, the end of life always comes as a shock.

With Ron at peace, we headed for the sun in a pre-arranged break for what was one of the most surreal holidays I have ever been on. Listening to Julie finalising funeral arrangements whist sat on a sun bed in Sicily is not the usually holiday activity and to be honest, the holiday was a blur. Life does throw up its own agenda as we continued to find out.

20th August 2017 - Back in the groove!

After a few weeks off, it's time to raise the bar on the 56notout challenge but I need your help!

I have a number of challenges in the diary but some are proving to be a little tricky and would appreciate your help.

As I have mentioned before, one of my favourite challenges is to run with 56 different people so if you fancy joining me for a run, drop me a message especially if you have already offered to run but we have not firmed up a date. Do you know someone famous who would like to join me for a few miles – how cool would that be and great publicity.

I need to drive something steam powered, must be someone out there with a steam roller? Drive a tank is on the list too.

Ringing church bells is on the list as well along with helping switch some Christmas lights on and I don't mean at home and yes I know it's only August.

One of my fears is heights and looking to give something climbing or abseiling a go, do you know of anyone that could help with that one?

"Good Evening Birmingham, will you please welcome XXXXX! " *It doesn't need to be Birmingham , but the challenge is to introduce a major artist or band at a big venue, any superstars out there?*

Any help appreciated and I am sure that Team 56notout have some other challenges up their sleeves for me but no more waxing if that's ok. I am at the spikey stage now but still have a body that looks like a young boy.

RUN #13 – SHARON BARRINGTON

With Ron's funeral behind us, life started to return to normal albeit with a massive void along with a change in routine for the family, it felt time to pick up the reins of the challenge. Sharon is a regular running companion of mine, but I know she would mind saying, can be a little cyclic and she is either running regularly with events in the diary or the trainers sit in the cupboard and gather dust. I do have the knack of persuading her to come out for a run and today was no exception. The last few months have been a rollercoaster for Sharon too and it was great to have a good catch up. Talk about the twist of fate and the belief in yourself and making your dreams come true, it was lovely to hear all about the new chapter in Sharon's life as she took on a new challenge and quantum leap going from catering manager to cabin crew, I could not have been more thrilled. I think that the full story is for Sharon to tell so will leave that to her. A lovely evening for a run around the Royal Borough and looking forward to a busy time ahead for both of us.

Meeting outside my old flat, it felt like old times so on such a beautiful evening, we took in the classic corners of this beautiful Regency gem and I am proud to be born here. The gardens are one of my favourite places in Leamington and in my option, the very heart and soul of this beautiful town. The park is where Leamingtonians meet to play, to talk, to run and unfortunately in these days to sleep. I love this place, so many memories from a young child feeding the ducks with my nan right up to now. Every time I come through those wrought iron gates, the memories come flooding back. Any time of year, the park always looks stunning, I love to see people taking advantage of this wonderful place. Popular dog walkers, mums and toddlers, dads and pushchairs, lovers, thinkers and runners of course. The park has not changed that much since my child hood, the aviary has swopped cages of exotic birds for overpriced coffee. I told Kathy of the floral clock from my youth, long gone now but I always live in hope that the soul still hides beneath the flower borders and in my lifetime will be brought back to life and enjoy being the centre of attention again. Under the watchful eye of the statue of Dr Jephson we record our "on run" video. The park was buzzing and good to see it alive on this summer's evening. A great run but the 56notout journal caught Sharon out and I still have a page waiting for her words of wisdom:-)

Run #14 – Kathy Healy

Welcome to a new day. I wanted to share with as many people as possible during the challenge year, the pleasure of a dawn run. To persuade some to get out of bed in what feels like the middle of the night is a big ask. To meet at 5.45am, inevitably the alarm goes of at 5am makes for a long day. The sun makes an appearance around 6 at this time of year so the dawn chorus was well underway and the darkness turning into daylight as we headed from the edge of town and out into the countryside. The morning delivered in spade loads and a short bit of trespassing to trig point TP5224 - Old Milverton, provided new and stunning views of the Warwickshire countryside, the path of the river Avon cloaked in mist emphasising the elevation and a breath-taking spectacle.

The chill of the night giving way to the potential promise of a glorious summers day, the sun bringing both warmth and an almost supernatural orange glow to nature. The effort of an early start was worth it and Kathy was hooked, we talked as we ran and it felt like the hectic world was put on hold and we could just enjoy the pleasure of seeing the arrival of a new day. I am in awe of the NHS and those who provide the care and support for those who need it, Kathy is one of those at the front line as a McMillan nurse and know that what she does is so much more than a 9 to 5 job and can be tough. I like Kathy's outlook on life and never without a smile, stopping mid run to take a photo of her with a random sunflower that had decided to grow and flourish in the middle of a field of wheat was fitting.

As with many of the people I run with, I enjoyed hearing Kathy's life story and what made her the person she is today.

I do love people and I am not sure I could live alone on an island.

Gone shootin'

I always pride myself that I have lead an active and varied life but something that seems the norm to many, like having my face painted, was a new experience for me. The same could be said about my next challenge. As a teenager, I had an air rifle, or a .177 mop gun as I remember it being called, the type of gun that was used in the shooting gallery. A legacy from the local fair that did the rounds of local towns in the autumn called the mop, but I had never fired a real gun. I thought this challenge would be not only easy to arrange and required little preparation plus done and dusted in an hour or so.

I was correct on the latter two but as for easy to arrange, I think not. In this age where health and safety rules the roost, the idea that I could just rock up somewhere a fire guns were a little optimistic, so I would need to enlist the help of someone in the know and as luck would have it, I knew just the man. Ex police firearm officer and trainer would fit the brief and a conversation was had with a friend from zero to hero would reinforce the potential complications of this challenge but wanting to support, David started thinking how he could help pull this off. The answer came from his gun club of which David was a committee member and someone where along the way, the idea of an open "bring a friend" type day was arranged.

The location of the gun club was buried deep in a wood in the Warwickshire countryside on the edge of an old World War Two aerodrome once home to brave RAF pilots and their flying machines. A pretty tricky place to find I was informed so David offered to swing past home so I could follow him to the venue for challenge number 9. On arriving in a clearing in the woods, I nervously followed David toward what were clearly ex-military buildings and to my first taste of the security of what surrounds guns these days. Introduced to the chair of the club and some form filling then to the heart of most clubs, the kitchen for a coffee.

Over a hot beverage, I found it increasingly easy to explain to the 56notout story and what brought me to this mysterious location to the small group of member and friends. David could sense my apprehension and was keen to explain the rules to protect my safety and those around me before donning ear protection and taking my place before the range and my first contact with a real gun. Starting with a handgun, we progressed from .177 air pistol to a rifle then .22 sporting rifle on to .357 under-lever rifle. Real guns with real bullets but today our prey would be inanimate paper targets so the potential power of the weapons still all too apparent. "Guns are designed for one thing Steve", David was clear to remind me - "to kill." A sport for sure to many but the bullet that came out the end of the barrel had no awareness as to whether the final destination was a paper target or something with a pulse. I soon learnt respect for these items and a very meaningful life lesson.

Considering this was my first encounter with a gun of any description for forty years and with not the best of eyesight, I did ok and when I had chance to fire David's pride and joy, a .177 Field Target Air Rifle I managed a bullseye at 20 metres and provided me with not only a great souvenir of a really interesting and thought provoking morning but also a great photo for my blog.

26th August 2017 - Respect

A busy week in the 56notout camp, with the next lot of challenges already in the diary, and have enjoyed a couple of runs, putting the world to rights, and enjoying the tail end of the summer.

Today saw the completion of challenge number 9, I had an old fairground air rifle when I was a kid but never fired anything more powerful, so with the help of David, and a local gun club, I had the chance to be let loose on something bigger. After a warm welcome and a chance to do my sales pitch, the time came to see if I could actually hit the target. Not too bad for a first attempt although my less then steady hand and poor eyesight did make the challenge interesting. What I did learn more than anything was respect, with the clear message that these weapons were designed for one thing and one thing only, to kill. I did go very quiet at one point, which many will find hard to believe as I realised that in the wrong hands, this combination of wood and metal, could bring a very different outcome. A big thankyou to all those concerned. Did not really think it would get to me as much as it did and thought it would just be a bit of fun. Maybe I think too deep or did this challenge give me a different perspective on what man can do to man. I will leave that with you.

Challenge, number 10, sees a different set of skills, along with Paddy from Helping Hands and team I will be attempting The Tempest Sportif , a 100 mile bike ride starting in Warwick and continuing through The Cotswold's , I wish I'd got the bike out more now !

We do have some fun stuff in the pipe line too with a chance to see how clever you lot think you are, but more about that in the next few weeks...

I am still looking for someone to trust me with a steam roller, and Daniel Craig still hasn't called, but there's still time, and there are plenty of runner places left if you fancy joining me for steady run and a natter as one of my 56 runners.

Enjoy the weekend folks and thanks for your support.

Run #15 – Sue Marshall

A kindred spirit, good friend and an avid fund raiser including Shelter, having already donned the red Shelter T shirt to run the London Marathon the previous year. As with many of our little running group, the support comes from within, people helping people. A concept clearly not new but I see more and more examples of this happening around me. I know that people are busier than ever these days, with increasing pressure from many angles but humans are essentially pack animals and helping people is an instinctive reaction. Sue typifies the people helping people philosophy, always doing good things to quote lady Diana :-

"Carry out a random act of kindness, with no expectation of reward, safe in the knowledge that one day someone might do the same for you."

Sue is relatively new to running but boy oh boy, that lady is focused. I dabble with a training plan but Sue follows hers to the letter and no surprise that the results show. But her focus does not stop with putting on her trainers, when fundraising, a big part of her motivation, I love the ingenious, varied and fun methods of extracting money from folks that she comes up with. The support from Sue's friends and family always gives me a warm feeling and always happy to step up and be Sue's quizmaster with some of her friends enjoying the competition and keeping me in check. With Sue having first-hand experience of marathon training, I am sure that we would run together in the new year, when along with many from the local running community, the start of a new year sees start of the dreaded marathon training. The time when normal life is handed over to the training schedule of almost daily runs and ever-increasing mileage of the weekly long run but today we could just enjoy the run and have a good chat.

RUN #16 – LUCY ROBERTS

Lucy is one of my success stories of life, another one of my 56notout runners that had a real tale to tell with life making her journey interesting to say the least and not for the first time in the book, I will leave the details of Lucy's journey when she writes the book of her own. We picked a good day to run and I had promised Lucy that I would take her on one of my favourite routes. The lanes and fields around old Milverton are special, time has forgotten this stunning part of Warwickshire and on my doorstep too, making it a regular stomping ground for me. It was good to introduce Lucy to the ducks as big as children and a killer rabbit the size of a family saloon. No idea of what I am talking about? Go to the beautiful hamlet of old Milverton and check out for yourself. This route is on my doorstep, my patch but this is somewhere new for Lucy and she loved it. The elevation, 65 metres above sea level, affords stunning views over the river valley complimented by the peace and tranquillity of the church of Saint James, leaving the church yard via the overflow burial area, the path leads to a small kissing gate hidden in the perimeter hedge. You cannot do anything but stop and stand in awe, the natural arch of the trees perfectly frames one of my favourite views in England. Although the warmth of a late summer afternoon made running an absolute pleasure, Lucy is winter baby and much prefers to run in the cooler weather. Providing another place to take her dog Benson for a walk, I was happy to share this little gem with her, making the "on run" video was easy but the selfie, that took a bit of taking.

On ya bike!

When I first made contact with Helping Hands, Lianne did offer to help me with some of the challenges on my list and early September I joined the team to take part in the Wiggle Tempest Sportive with the opportunity to ride my bike in the beautiful Warwickshire countryside with a number of distances on offer. I opted for the 100km, with Paddy and Tom going for the big one, 100 miles. Julie, Carol, Pete, Alistair and Lorraine had already signed up for the 33 miler, I opted for the middle distance, 100k would be far enough for me today. Standing along with the Helping Hands banner before we headed off made a great photograph and highlighted the comradeship of the HH family. As we all headed off together to the start, I didn't realise that this would be the last I would see of the team. Paddy and Tom, both keen cyclists soon headed off with 100 miles ahead of them and I soon lost the others in the first few miles. I really wanted to do the big one with Tom and Paddy, a distance that has always eluded me.

I have got close a few times but never managed to get to this magical number, one day maybe. For the rest of the ride, I was cycling pretty much solo, cycling can be pretty lonely at times and plays on my dislike of being on my own. I like to surround myself with people and love the company of others. Although I have a brother and sister, the age difference almost made my childhood one of an only child but have none of the traits that many only children have. I like a crowd and in most times in my life, when I have done a solo activity, whether sport, travel or just arriving alone at a function, I soon strike up a conversation and join forces with someone.

Very different to my wife Julie, who loves and craves her own space.

Although I did speak to people as we cycled along, the nature of the route along the leafy country lanes did not really lend itself to social cycling so just sat back and enjoyed the stunning scenery. I had a heathy piece of bread pudding that I had bought the previous day and when I hit 56 miles, I promised myself a rest stop and a private celebration. The route took in some stunning Warwickshire scenery tickling the fringes of the Cotswolds with the tell-tale houses built from the tell-tale golden stone. The signs to Warwick along with familiar places came as a welcome boost and heading into the finish at Warwick racecourse I felt happy with my days' work and another challenge in the bag.

Realising the importance of keeping the world informed of my exploits, I took some photographs and posted a video on social media having first calling into base camp to let Julie know that I had survived to live another day. A steady cycle home to a refreshing shower and a cuppa, the best prize of all.

With all the team home safe and sound with news of everyone's achievements was lovely to hear and the offer of a beer with Paddy, although tempting, would have to wait for another day with life yet again having other ideas.

2nd September 2017 - Be prepared?

Another busy week in the 56notout camp, more of my 56 runs and the first of the cycling challenges. I was never a boy scout but I do understand the motto " be prepared "… I wasn't ! today's cycle ride was 109k around the beautiful Warwickshire countryside and a bit of other counties too. I wish I had put a few more training miles in, it was a tough one, but did give me plenty of time to ponder life and think about the months ahead. For most of the ride I was on my own, so the motivation had to come from within. Seeing some stunning views and lovely little villages made me realise that life is always better when you have someone to share it with. Planet Earth can be one lonely place if you are on your own and the power of being in a team delivers the best results. Seeing the great work that people do when they join forces always warms my heart and continues to be my motivation and those in the 56notout family.

Not a challenge, but going to be a great fun is the 56notout quiz night extravaganza that Emma has organised on the 18th November 2017 , I for one am really looking forward to the night. Not because I get to see the Coventry Pub Quiz Legend – Bolo in action, or hearing the talented Eva Pemberton perform, but a night off from any challenges and a chance to have a bit of fun – a great team effort and I am lucky that I have so many people helping and supporting me, you are much appreciated.

The tickets are going fast so those folks not on Facebook let me know and I will get the details to you.

The bike ride would set me up for my trip to Belgium the following weekend. Not part of the challenge directly but the annual cycling long weekend away in Europe maybe it would give me chance to run in a few cities.

Run #17 – Jane Bates

With summer in its final stages, I wanted to enrol another member to my unofficial dawn runners club. Globetrotting Jane was more than happy to run with me but did take a little bit persuading to leave a nice warm bed and head out into the cooler late summer morning and see the arrival of a new day. The change in the length of days always seems to become more apparent as you head into September, meeting at 5.45am, twilight was some 15 minutes away and we started our run in darkness but the colour of sky changing from deep blue to orange tinted aqua as the sun hinted of its pending arrival. I had a route in mind that would bring us to Kenilworth Castle from the northwest, away from the road and urbanisation affording the lesser known but in my opinion, the most spectacular view of the castle ruins especially bathed in the early morning sun. I like Jane and always good company to run with even if she does keep telling me that I drink too much. Have I convinced Jane that the dawn is the best time the day, to be honest, I would say not, time will tell.

From the words Jane wrote in my journal, I reckon the run was worth getting out of bed for.

It's all about the bike ....

To mis quote Lance Armstrong, the title of his 2000 autobiography "It's Not About the Bike" (well worth a read, whatever your opinion of this disgraced athlete) however, with the chance to run in two cities it was too good an opportunity not to miss. We were on mainland Europe for our annual lads cycling trip having tested our lacking mechanical skills with an epic bike tear down and rebuild extravaganza courtesy of Eurostar we travelled from Lille to our base for three nights, the stunning Belgian city of Bruges. These annual trips to the continent with Rob, Paul and Nigel started back in 2014 when we took the 406km Avenue Verte from London to Paris and now are a regular slot in the diary each year. This is our second visit to Belgium but the first time cycling in and around Bruges. Having a base makes the cycling easier for at least the middle couple of days when we don't have to ride with panniers carrying our worldly goods.

For me this is my third visit to the beautiful city, the first time in the late eighties on route to friend's wedding in Germany (forgetting my shirt if I recall and having to try and buy a new one en route was a challenge in itself but if my memory serves me correct, good old C&A came to the rescue) , the second in 2014 for our honeymoon when a daily run around the medieval city a regular feature in the daily itinerary along with getting lost. I wanted to try and fit in a short run before breakfast if I could but not to far as I did have a bit of cycling to do and I did not want to get lost but with our hotel in sight of the main square, going off piste was less likely. On the day of the run, we planned to head to the coast and into Holland to add another country to the trip so a busy day ahead.

The early morning streets are magical and the smell of freshly baked bread making me hungry and ready for the best meal of the day. The last time I ran in Bruges was just before Christmas, wrapped up with hat and gloves exploring the cold and misty cobbled streets with a festive scene at every turn, but today, at the tail end of the summer with the kids only just back at school for the start of a new academic year, the weather was good with a pair of shorts and t shirts replacing winter attire. The impressive squares drenched in late summer morning sun made the buildings glow like on fire and so peaceful, the tiny streets taking a breath before the hordes of tourists arrived on mass to sample the beer and buy chocolate, take a boat trip or ride majestically in a horse drawn carriage. Having done all these activities and many more in my previous visits, I just enjoyed a gentle jog around the empty streets before getting back on the bike but not before I had eaten my body weight in breakfast goodies ready for the day in the saddle. City #4 ticked off the list.

The final day of our four day adventure takes the gang back to France and the city of Lille to catch the Eurostar train back to Blighty and home. As on the outward journey, this involves dismantling bikes and packing them into flight cases with the promise of rebuilding then once back in London before a race across the city to catch the train to Coventry for the final leg of the trip. I am never a big fan of the last day with the pressure of the clock to ensure connections are made so we always allow plenty of time just in case of punctures or unforeseen delays so arriving in Lille on plan and the bikes safely in their flight cases, we had more than enough time for the traditional end of trip beer in the Grand Place in the centre of this city at the northern tip of France on the border with Belgium. Before I dived into my beer, I took the opportunity to run in city number 5, a bonus for the challenge list however my video blog gave the first indication that the idea to go 56 days without a shave or haircut was not going to be well received by at home or the office.

Travelling light, shaving equipment is an unnecessary addition to the packing list so by the end of the four days, we all look a little less than our best and the comments from those close to me started me thinking. Within days, this planned challenge of going un-groomed for 56 days was aborted.

RUN #18 – IAN YARDE

I run with Ian most weeks and is very much part of my weekly routine so I wanted him to be one of my 56. He would be joining me for a challenge before the month was over when we competed against each other in my debut triathlon but this morning it was all about the run. We have ran the streets of Leamington and Warwick many times before and passing a temporary home in a shop doorway a regular reminder of the issues facing others. I remember running with Ian earlier in the year and remarked that in this day and age no one should be without a roof over their heads and mid run, as Ian and I were having a good old rant about home, work, life in no particular order, we came across someone asleep in a shop doorway or curled up under a canal bridge, we go quiet and the conversation changes...... This particular run stays with me and the thoughts are filed away for something in the future maybe – the seed is planted and lay dormant ready for the time to start to grow. Its only January but today's run is going to change my life, you are going to have to wait until the end of the year to find out more but remember today, I will.

The one good thing about running with others is the commitment, what's in the diary generally gets done and it's oh so easy to lose the battle of the bed when no one is waiting on your doorstep or on a street corner. I love running with others not only for the company, I love people but also for the commitment. Once the arrangements are made, generally I will be there. It has got to be something serious for me not to show up, but a different kettle of fish if I am running solo. Without that promise or commitment, I will look for any excuse to stay in bed but once I've put those trainers on and got out there, I am always glad I did; same goes for exercise of any shape or form.

You have got to love those endorphins, but I still think the best part of exercise is when it stops but always feel better for having done something physical.

OUT OF MY DEPTH

The challenge was to swim in open water but a mile, nobody ever said anything about swimming a mile!

Water is a big fear of mine, on the very first morning of the 56notout year, I mentioned that I was having early morning training sessions to improve my swimming, waste of time. I am not a swimmer and not something I feel I wanted to put the time into but I know that practice would make a big difference but the morning training session did go West so for the next challenge it would all be about how we did on the day. My fear of water goes all the way back to my childhood, everyone had swimming lessons with my junior school, Cashmore, and every week, we would head down to Leamington baths. The pool opened in 1890 and closed 1989 the swimming pool was closed and relocated to a new leisure centre building in Newbold Comyn. I would not like to hazard a guess how many local children learnt to swim at these Victorian baths as we called them but I was not one them. Learning to swim would happen very much later in my life, early twenties if my memory serves me well.

The challenge was open water swimming but Julie had other ideas. If the challenge was going to mean anything then it would have to be something to remember. Organised by the same organisers that make the London Marathon a seamless event, Swim Serpentine looked like a good event to take part in but a mile in chilly water in the middle of London. I like the idea of the enormity of a big event but with no training under my belt and untried kit was not a good combination.

Many challenges I was on my own but for this one I had company and so glad I did. When Julie signed me up for

2017, she signed up for both of us so I would not be alone. The days before the event were a real rollercoaster of emotions, when the race packs arrived the reality of what lay ahead became all too real. Together we weighed up the options, we had spent a small fortune on wet suits, entry fees and travel which I did not want to waste but I was nervous and we were very unprepared which is not a good combination. As We ran through the options, the stubborn side of Julie became apparent, failure was not an option and it was clear that we were in this together so play or pass it was both or neither, but I knew I needed to get this done or the challenge would remain un-achieved and I feared failure. The "Swim Serpentine" team did a great job on social media for generating the excitement. Daily videos from race director Colin Hill gave a taste of what was ahead and news that the water temperature was now 15 degrees so wet suits were optional as the water was warm enough. The average bath water at home is between 38 to 41 degrees so like taking a bath it would not be. The scale of lake in Hyde park was starting to sink in, the Serpentine Lake or Serpentine River as it is sometimes called is over 5 metres deep in places so I would be out of my depth in more ways than one.

Advice was offered by close friends who had the experience that we lacked but one thing no one could help with was the lack of time and preparation. The first time Julie and I tried on the wetsuits were the day before and not in water so leaving no room for any problems. Getting my less than athletic body into the neoprene suit was tough enough in the comfort of our own home but on the day, we would have to dress in public and look like we knew what we were doing. Some of the great advice I did take, plastic bags on the feet to help get the un flattering wet suit on and anti-chaffing cream around the arm pits / neck put into to place but I was still worried about the challenge ahead and as I left the changing tent surrounded by folks that seemed a lot more relaxed than I was and very glad to be reunited with my soul mate and swim companion.

The video log before the start was one of the funniest when looking like something from a bad sci-fi film as I announced to the world that I was "shitting it" as I was. "Get yourselves in water before the start mate", a veteran of the event told us. It was cold and the thought of getting in the chilly water and then back out to get back in did not sound like a good idea but before I knew it I was heading to the "dunk zone" closely followed by Julie. I am glad we did as I could hyper ventilate in private and get used to the cold water that would be home for the next hour or so. The less than flattering orange swimming caps marked the very last wave of the day and taking our place at the back so as to have a clear vision of the way ahead the race was underway. I had my escape route planned and looking for a short cut across the lake but the marshal in the supporting canoe was having none of it and I was glad. Out of my depth and in less than clear water I soon got into a rhythm, I was bloody swimming in open water and so far so good.

The maiden outing of the suit was going ok, not the same could be said for Julie whose ill-fitting wet suit was hindering her progress. A strong swimmer and very confident in the water, she later described the effects of eBay's finest was like swimming with armbands on your wrists and ankles and not positioning well in the water. Ever the trooper, and not wanting to give me any excuse to stop, she pressed on. Seeing that she had acquired her personal safety canoe, I pressed on to get this out of the way. Progress was slow with only the occasional swan as company who made it look easy. The field had pretty much left a clean set of heals as we rounded the first set of buoys marking the west end of the Serpentine with its restaurant where we had eaten a pre-swim snack earlier in the day with now only a hand full of swimmers at the back of the wave.

By the time I had reached about the half way point, both Julie and I had our personal escorts. We chatted about anything and everything, slowly but surely I progressed though the water periodically checking on Julie via our canoe based guardians. Reaching the opposite end of the lake I realised I still had some way to go and I did not need a short but sharp attack of cramp but my canoe buddy was on hand to assist and was soon on my way again, glancing back, I could see the first set of buoys that we had passed what felt like a life time ago, deflated and heading for the shore to be packed up for future events. Support at the finish had dwindled but support there was, race director Colin announcing my arrival as if I was the first man home.. Beaching on the carpeted ramp and with a life guard under each arm, I was unceremoniously oiked out of the water and on to my feet. I found out later that this undignified procedure was provided to all swimmers, whether elite or beginners, ongoing under the finish board were treated with the same inelegant exit from the water.

Once my race was over and back on terra firma I was told to get my wetsuit off my upper body to stop getting too cold, my time would remain a mystery as my timing chip had fallen off pretty much as soon as I entered the water. Waiting on the finish pontoon, I cheered my baby on the final straight and longed to get warm. A finishing swimmer, just in front of Julie was clearly suffering from the cold and thought she was in Leeds promptly the recipient of some medical attention. Proud of our achievement against all odds, I was really happy to see Julie wrapped in Swim Serpentine towel, usually given to the elite swimmers, with a glass of fizz from the diehard supporters, who had clapped everyone home, thanks folks.

And into the hot tub, the only one working as this late stage of the day but saved for the final finishers. The water might have been a little lived in but it felt amazing and the icing on the cake, an "in hot tub "medal presentation.

Changing into warm clothes in a deserted, but very well heated tent was a great feeling. What a day, home James with another challenge done and a fear overcome, I could not have done this without my lady and the Swim Serpentine crew.

16th September 2017 - Walk the footsteps of a stranger

Music is a big part of my life and came across a song in the last few weeks, the words got to me and made to think. The song was Colours of the Wind from the Disney film Pocahontas.

> *You think the only people who are people*
> *Are the people who look and think like you*
> *But if you walk the footsteps of a stranger*
> *You'll learn things you never knew, you never knew*

The 56 not out challenge has really given me a chance to meet some amazing people and also walk in the footsteps of strangers. What most of us take for granted, for some is life changing. A hot bath and a change of clothes can make such a difference to someone living on the streets. I was moved by Demi's story from the Helping Hands Facebook page, and wish her all the best for the future.

I had planned to go without a shave or a haircut for 56 days but only after a short time the change in my appearance was already raising eyes and attracting comments. The expectation of a clean and tidy image does effect on the way people treat you, working in a profession organisation I would not have lasted much longer before someone would have had "a little chat". The length of my hair and the grey beard did not have any impact on the quality of my work and is all about the perception so can fully understand that for a person down on their luck can soon become a downward spiral.

So as the challenges continue, I can not only see where the money goes but also that the help is around if you need it, but it will not land in your lap.

This weekend, with my wife Julie, I took on one of my biggest challenges. I hate water; I am rubbish at swimming and most of all, hate being out of my depth. So to take on open water swimming was a big ask and to say I was frightened was an understatement, but we did it, swam a mile in open water. A big thank you to the Colin and the Swim Serpentine team and everyone who gave us help and support. The best bit, getting clean, having a hot soak afterwards, and getting some clean clothes on. It makes you feel human again, how must have Demi and all the others making use of Helping Hands new bathing facilities have felt?

Sometimes you don't appreciate what we consider to be the small things.

RUN #19 – SIOBHAN CAINES

After such a busy day, a lie in would have been lovely but that was not on the agenda for me though, it was Sunday morning I had a new person to run with and I was excited. The anticipation is the best part for me, what will they be like, what happens if they are super fit and expecting a session with a real athlete, but I am pretty good a sounding people out and to be honest my life is an open book and clear what I am about. My runner this morning, number 19 was another work colleague of Emma and it was great to meet Siobhan Caines. I think we both were a little apprehensive, not quite knowing how our run would go. Siobhan was lovely, bubbly and full of life. We did a few laps of her local park and as we ran, the conversation flowed. We talked of our lives, our hopes and dreams and of course the challenge year. I loved hearing about Siobhan's plans and after our run, I felt like had known her for years. I hoped that we had made a connection and one day, I will get a call to say, I have done it, I have ran my marathon or something even better and who knows I might have just played a tiny part in making it happen.

Run #20 – Kate Evans

I like Kate, always a smile and a positive comment whenever we bumped into each other. In recent years, Kate has switch her allegiance from running to rowing but throwing herself into the new sport as she did with her running. Occasionally we have a chance and albeit fleeting contact on a weekend run when I catch a glimpse of Kate in a rowing boat with myself on the river bank in the local park. I was really pleased when she offered to put on the trainers and join me for a steady trot around our home town. Kate lives in Warwick too but on the other side of town, so we decided to meet mid-point. On meeting, Kate said she had to do a short detour and pick up something from the boat house on route. I had never been to the rowing club before and I stood, jaw dropping at the impressive sight of Warwick Castle from the water's edge. Kate could see I was taken back "you should give this rowing a try" and offered to get me out on the water. I was excited and thrilled to have a challenge that I had not considered added to the growing list along with the offer of help to make it happen.

Leaving the club, I was buzzing, not only was I having a lovely run around the town I am so happy to call home with a great friend, but I had the potential of a great challenge on the list. I couldn't help but run though Warwick market, dodging between Saturday shoppers and market stalls, with a quick "hello" to my favourite fruit and veg team. As we ran, I could tell that Kate loved her town as well, lucky to life in a beautiful part of the world, all that is missing is the sea.....

I liked Kate's comment in my journal

"I shall plan an outing on the river for us (so keep practicing the swimming.....)

Let's make the running a regular thing - at least once a year"

I like your style Kate and it's a deal.

23rd September 2017 - Are we there yet?

Nearly a third of the way through the 56notout year, it's about time for an update.

Of the 56 challenges, 11 are complete with another 3 started. Unfortunately, 2 of the 3 will not see completion until nearer the end of the challenge year but look out for the "Street life" calendar which should be on sale in time for Christmas. Cycling 100k was hard with little training and the swim the serpentine day, which was a one-mile swim around the Serpentine in London pushed me way out of my comfort zone. Some more challenges that are coming up in the next few weeks include my first ever Triathlon on Sunday, the ketchup outfit is coming out again for the Birmingham Half Marathon in October, a fire walk and the chance to experience life on the streets as I spend the night outside at the end of November. I also plan to do Parkrun blindfolded before the end of the year and hopefully drive a JCB.

I am getting new challenges all the time so open to suggestions but no more waxing if that's ok folks!

Fancy being one of my 56notout runners, just let me know.

So far the challenge has raised nearly £1000 for the two charities Helping Hands and Shelter with more to come from the Quiz Night in November, still some tickets available.

Back in the water

Just over a week since our little swim around the Serpentine, I was back in a swimming costume, a trisuit to be precise and equally as unflattering. I hoped that last week's swim would put me in good shape for the swimming part of the event and being pool based would be a little water and at least I could see the bottom however racing was a different kettle of fish. I had new disciplines to master and already the banter and speculation had started as to the result in our own three horse race. I was the dark horse with no previous form so an accurate prediction would be tricky. I was confident that the swim would be the deciding factor but my confidence in the water, or lack of very clear along with my lack of knowing the intricacies of a new sport, what to do and importantly what not to do in transition, getting trainers on with wet feet, talc sorts that out, cycling in wet clothes and I was nervous fear of the unknown and a bit of pressure from Ian and Richard, my support team for today. Both had done triathlons before so I was feeling very much the new boy, I took guidance from these gents regarding start positions. Thinking the best plan was to start together at least to give me a little moral support at the start which I appreciated.

Registration done and numbers issued, like my first day at school I closely followed the others, race number tattoo on the arm, bike and helmet, talc in the trainers and bike and kit laid out for a speedy change from swimmer to cyclist.

Taking a minute or two to do a video log to post on social media and a few photos to remember the day in my old age, I couldn't help thinking we looked like we were off to a "only gay in the village" contest. No one looks good in Lycra I convinced myself and was glad I opted for a 56notout T shirt over my trisuit for the cycle and run in the name of good PR but did not help with my appearance for the swim.

Heading for the pool, the nerves were apparent, I felt surrounded by elite athletes and the fact that this was my debut appearance pretty obvious. Lining up pool side in numerical order and in earshot of Richard and Ian, the memories of the start line in Hyde park coming flooding back but this time cold water was exchanged for competition. Watching earlier competitors start did not help me feel any better. The swim was 12 lengths of a 33-metre pool, roughly 400 metres with each swimmer setting off at five second intervals. You started in the water so at least I did have to contend with some heroic dive off the starting block in full view of the world. As we stood poolside in numerical order in an ever reducing line it was soon my turn, my stomach churned as competitor 288 was counted off, then it was my turn to enter the water. 289 - five, four, three, two, one, go and I was on my way.

The next quarter of an hour felt like a lifetime as I bobbed, ducked and avoided the other swimmers that seemed hell bent in drowning me. I had swam about three feet before I heard the five, four, three, two, one go count down of the next competitor and in a breath, number 290 was invading my space and soon I was surrounded by arms and legs all wanting my piece of water and shoving me out of the way. I never thought I would ever say it but give me cold deep water any day of the week and the space that goes with it. 400 metres and 15 minutes 13 seconds later I emerged from the pool feeling like I had just climbed out of a washing machine. I had had enough already as I threw my swimming cap in the poolside bucket and strolled the damped walkways to be reunited with my trusty steed. Ian and Richard had long gone and I was glad to see Sue on the balcony of the pool with my heart very clearly on my sleeve. She later told me that my face was a picture and pretty apparent that I was not having a good time as I climbed out of the water and didn't expect to see me taking up the sport and she was spot on. Climbing on my bike and glad of the dry t shirt to at least cut down the wind chill I knew that this would be my one and only triathlon. It's the swimming. I don't mind the bike and run at all, it's the swimming, I think you get that now......

The 16 km route on the whole was good, an area I know, pretty villages with a nice climb to get you out of your saddle and a chance to battle with the traffic on the main road into Stratford on Avon but at least I didn't have elbows in my face and enjoyed the chance to sit down and enjoy my own space. I did have my chain come off to keep me on my toes doing a speedy bit of roadside maintenance to the back drop of Sunday motorists head to Shakespeare's birthplace. The arrival back at transition for the last time was a relief, just a case of stowing my bike and losing the cycling helmet and off for a run by the river.

Back to having company and the only aggression was from local dog walkers who insisted on having their dogs on a 10-foot retractable lead poised to up end any would be runner and a real pet hate of mine. Completely oblivious to the ongoing race, Sunday strollers adding to the fun and providing a welcome distraction. Before long, I was heading to the finish line to complete my first and last triathlon, ticking off another challenge and learning yet more about myself and what gets under my skin. Video blog done and a call home, I was ready for a cuppa, a bit of cake and to swop race stories with my two race buddies. "Fancy another one Steve?" Let me think - No!

Trisuit anyone? I do have one for sale if anyone is interested, warn once.

And the results are in, no real surprises.....

A great experience but not one that I want to repeat any time soon.

RUN #21 – VINCE TAYLOR

The class of 77, had to be done. I work with Vince but we go back a lot further than a recent work colleague. We went to the same school and in the same year but not in the same class. Our secondary school, Myton High had a huge catchment area and I think Vince and I were at opposite extremes of the map. We catch up occasionally at Leamington Parkrun where Vince once described me as his nemesis and when we run, the friendly banter flows. Today, the pressure was off and it was all about the pleasure of the run. Meeting at the top of our home town, the obvious choice was to head across the fields to old Milverton, always a favourite place to run. Over thirty years since we left school and headed out into the big wide world, it's nice to be with a kindred spirit who shares the passion for our home town. Vince is a fanatical Leamington Football Club Supporter, the Brakes as they are better known locally, paying homage to Leamington's major employer, Lockheed who's factory dominated the area opposite the old Windmill Ground, home to the team from the 1930's until the late 80's when the need of houses in Thatcher's Britain moved the team out of town. I love to see Vince's love of the sport and as always wearing the football top. We talk of old faces and recall names from the old school days pondering the people that have just disappeared off the radar. Life can be like that and dialogue as we run, peels away the years and after a few miles, it feels like the 1970's again and back to the days when life was far less complicated. Together we grow up at the tail end of the Vietnam War, the Cuban Missile crisis and the Cold War, when I talk to my girls about when Frankie goes to Hollywood sing about the Two Tribes the memories come flooding back. I remember the booklet dropping through the door to educate the homes of Britain on how to survive a nuclear attack – bloody hell! Not forgetting the Miners' Strike, the three day week and Margret Thatcher aka Thatcher the Snatcher stopping our free milk back in 1971, I often wonder how we all ended up being so well balanced .....

RUNNING BLIND

You must have done this sometime in your life, either on your own or with others? Asked yourself losing which of the senses, would you hate the most? Having had the benefit of a full set, most people can make an educated decision. Sight, sound, hearing, touch and smell, maybe a sixth sense if I wanted to push the envelope a little, but for me sight is up there with a tough one to lose and a fear of losing control that would inevitably go with it. With the help of Ellen who I had met at the Two Castles earlier in the year, I was going to be given the chance to have a life changing experience and have a taste of what it would be like to lose my sight. To get a good flavour of what it would be like to put trust in the hands of another in a public place along with a great chance to do some PR and get the 56notout challenge word out there, I planned to run blindfolded at a local park run. Stratford on Avon, where I had only done my first and last triathlon the weekend before. In the interim week, Ellen had arranged for guide runner to look after me as she was race director at the weekly event and in the days running up to big day, the name of my eyes was declared. I think you know him Steve, it's Chris Spriggs, I did. My blog mentor from earlier in the year, a good guy and someone I knew I could put my trust in for the three laps of the town park. On arriving at the venue, I felt nervous, again I was stepping into the unknown, handing over control along with the loss of a main sense. Chris ran through the guide instructions, what he would say and do along with my first introduction to the cord that would be the physical bond between us as we ran. As Ellen did her welcomes and all important safety briefing, I stood in silent anticipation, blindfold on my forehead. I wanted to stay sighted as long as possible. Reality structure as Ellen warned the other participants that we have a "blind runner" on the course today along with a brief explanation. A round of applause signalled the time to "go blind" and head to the start.

My weekly blog says it all.

30th September 2017 - A different perspective!

When I started this journey of challenges, I wanted to put myself in the shoes of others and see life from a different perspective. I have seen Maggie, who is blind, at park run a few times and have always been in awe of her determination and outlook on life, wondering how running must feel when bereft of the sense of sight. Having met Maggie and her guide Ellen at the Two Castles back in June, I mentioned that blind running was one of my challenges but would need a bit of help. How could they resist a grown man dressed as a bottle of ketchup ?! although Maggie did suggest that maybe we should not run together as that would not work, gotta love her sense of humour!

So today, with Ellen helping me to make the arrangements I completed challenge #13 with my good friend Chris as my guide. The blindfold went on and with me hanging tightly to the guide cord; we headed to the start line. Chris explained the instructions I would be given such as countdown to change of surface, high knees when I needed to lift my feet a little higher and the promise of a running commentary of everything around me. The first thing that amazed me was that only after a few steps my remaining senses went into overdrive with my hearing, smell and spatial awareness filling the gaps in my new sightless world. I could hear the birds in the trees above me and an approaching wheel chair sounded like a juggernaut so with my absolute trust in Chris to keep me safe I kept the back of my cord hand as one with Chris's forearm, (no doubt leaving a damp patch on his top)with this close contact, I felt more at ease.

The support from passing runners and those who we past (yes we passed people) was touching and pushed us on to the finish, each lap feeling better than the last as I adapted to my new world.

The finish was a welcome "sight" and the cheers on the run in had me in tears.

Those 35 mins 49 secs in the shoes of a blind runner has changed my perspective forever and given me yet another view of lives of others. Give it a try if you get chance and you will see life in a different way.

A big thank you to Ellen, Chris, Sue and everyone at Stratford Parkrun – pity I missed out on the cake.

An amazing experience and one I would talk about for a long time to come. I learnt respect for people like Maggie, who have no choice than to put themselves in the hands of others but also I learnt that in life, you can take nothing for granted but also how fantastic the human body is in the way a change in conditions, results in a near immediate adaptation and compensation - perfection. Removing the blind fold at the finish, returning to a complete suite of senses nearly had me flat on my face as I became disorientated with the overload of data.

Run #22 – Shazli Cooke

It's always good to have someone with medical knowledge to run with, cutting out all that waiting time and having to book an appointment. Only joking but having a doctor as a friend does come in handy sometimes and I am fortunate to have a plethora of medical people in my team. Shazli is a regular runner at the Sunday group but with a full time job and children always heading in different directions, being a doctor, a mum, a wife etc. has got to be tough. A very common thread with many if not most of the people I run with these days and when we do get to run, I feel that we are all glad of the headspace. Running does give you that and a chance to just "be" for a while. I am not sure you get the same when running on a treadmill in a gym but that's only my opinion. To run with someone on a Saturday morning was a break from the norm and made a nice change.

We mixed it up a little with a combination of quiet streets and country lanes, it looked like most of Kenilworth was having a lie in as the town was quiet. It's been a long time since I have had a lie in, I like the mornings which is a pretty good job really as my body clock is programmed for a dawn get up, approximately 5/5.30 am oblivious to seasons or day of the week. If I manage to stay in bed until 7am then I have done well. Meeting at 8 at a weekend was not a problem. Shazli is one of those people who just gets on with it, nothing seems to phase her. I ran a half marathon with Shazli who had a bad back, not a problem, a few pain killers and off we went. We had a good run and ran most of the 13.1 miles together until the call of nature split us up. I love the East meets West fusion that Shazli brings to life, a great run and a pleasure to get out of bed for.

7th October 2017 - The luxury of choice

An interesting week in the 56notout camp, I continue to be moved by the support and help for this crazy year. The quiz night is shaping up to be a great night, looking forward to seeing you all. We still have a few tickets left and if you have signed up to come, if you have already paid, thank you and if you haven't got round to it yet , in the words of Tom Cruise , " show me the money " ! We already have some great raffle prizes, thanks to local business and the powers of persuasion from the crew. If you can help with any more, let us know or bring them along on the night.

Last week's challenge got a lot of people talking, which was one of the aims for this year, but like a lot of the challenges I have taken on, and some of those yet to come, I have a choice.

I heard a song in the week that I hadn't heard for a while and got it me thinking. The song was Common People by PULP.

Rent a flat above a shop
Cut your hair and get a job
Smoke some fags and play some pool
Pretend you never went to school
But still you'll never get it right
Cause when you're laid in bed at night
Watching roaches climb the wall
If you called your dad he could stop it all

When the challenge is done, I have a choice. Take off the blindfold and I can see, have a night on the streets and in the morning return home to a hot shower and a nice warm bed. Not everyone has that choice, I am very fortunate to give these things a try, out of my comfort zone for sure, but with a safety boat or support crew a call away and at any time I can call for help. What would I think about taking on some of these challenges if there was no safety net? That would put a whole new angle on it, what would it be like to have these problems every day? Food for thought....

Back in the bottle

As the autumn started to show signs of becoming winter, the ketchup outfit was ready for another outing. This time taking to the streets of the second city, twice the distance and with the addition of spicy mustard aka my eldest daughter Libby. The bright yellow outfit had already gone through 56notout brand transformation from Sue's mum and with the addition of some yellow tights, we were ready. I had already learnt that putting the tights on is the toughest part of getting ready. On race day decided to do that in the comfort of my own home; the thought of balancing on one leg in public was something I wanted to avoid, but this came at a price. I would have to walk from home to the local railway station and then travel in on the train in red tights and short shorts. As you can imagine I did get some odd glances, not as bad on the train as it was pretty obvious with the number of runners about that an event was going on, but strolling down the street was a different thing altogether. I favoured the back streets rather than the main road for obvious reasons as the looks from passing cars did nothing for my street credibility!

I had arranged to meet Libby at Moor Street Station, then in to our outfits then on to the start. I wanted to greet her as ketchup man so finding a quiet corner of the platform, I made the transformation. As I appeared on the platform, the glances turned to smiles and the requests for a photo started. I love the attention and reckon all publicity is good. Libby and Tim's face was a picture when they got off the train and once in her outfit, the fun started. We both love the limelight and knew we were in for a fun day.

As I have been running for a good few years, I know a few people in the community, so the start of any event ends up being a bit of a reunion and today was no exception. We met up with friends and it was good to have a catch up with Ali, along with a few photos. Once in the start pens, having said our farewells to the support crew, we all have our little rituals. 'Do we need the loo?' always a prominent thought, but I always make time to think of my Mum and pray for her to look out for us. Libby was quieter too, "it's 13 miles' dad and not to be taken lightly" and she is right. People start races with the intention of crossing the finish line and sadly some folks do not see the end. Respect the distance and do all you can to be ready and minimise the risk.

We were ready, a hug and off we went. Today's event was different, the organisers had a marathon and half marathon running pretty much the same route, but with a staggered start time which tried to ensure that the majority of runners finished, whether full or half around the same sort of time. Which meant that as we undertook our distance, people would be on the course with a good few miles already behind them. We started with our friend Ali, but the day was not going well for her and on route we left her to run her own race and take the pressure off us all. The crowd were amazing and where the public lined the streets, boy did we milk the attention. High fives and selfies made the miles fly by. As we approached the final few miles, we met a friend of Libby's, Tom who had completed the marathon and now was doing the half on top because he could! Total respect for Tom, who was running to raise money for St Giles Hospice in Birmingham and was still going strong. I think the chat did us all good, and with a captive audience and a chance to spread the word spurring us all on to the finish line.

As we ran towards the city and the growing skyline, the desire to finish grew ever closer. Exercise is great but better when it stops. On route we played the crowd, we high five'd, we stopped for photos, we did the whole nine yards and we were having a ball. Libby is a chip of the old block as they say when it comes to people and great to spend some time together.

The run into the finish was never ending, uphill, always a favourite but with the final run in comes the crowds and the cheers. The last 200 metres of an event is always the best. With the finish in sight, the support is amazing and roar of the spectators deafening and the emotion always gets to me, generally crossing the line in tears. Libby, looking fresh as a daisy as always, was lapping up the attention, sweeping and weaving towing me along with her enthusiasm. Crossing the line, the watch stopped, we hug and it's all over. 13.1 miles - done and another challenge off the list and another city too. I guess I could have counted Libby as one of my 56 runners but we had another date for that one, a little more significant but you will have wait until the following summer to hear more about my run with my first born. An impromptu conversation on the platform with a lady who had come to cheer her daughter made me think and give me an idea for my weekly blog. Just for the record, Ali finished the race and was not far behind us, very happy to cross the finish line. City number 6 and another challenge off the list.

16th October 2017 - Both sides of the fence

Another challenge done and was lovely to have some company for this one. The day was a fabulous opportunity to spread the word and awareness of the issues faced by our homeless people and who could resist a man in tights. The walk to the station was certainly interesting and turned a few heads. Arriving at the station was amazing and the 56notout logo will feature in a lot of people race day memories. But in a conversation with a family at the station, this lovely lady said I don't run but love to come and support. It made me realise that without the support and the buzz of the crowd, this would have just been another run.

Thank you, Birmingham, and Libby you were amazing.

Run #23 – Dave Lancaster

Nice to meet a kindred spirit, Dave was Julie's friend and when they met, she knew I would like this guy. We didn't run but for a change, we walked or "twalked" as Dave calls it. Suiting Dave's return to fitness, the combination of a talk and walk was nice and provided the chance to chat whilst exploring Warwickshire's stunning countryside. We chatted about life and its meaning, life guru's and snake oil salesmen. I liked this guy, he was real and liked where he was heading. Dave was on an amazing journey of his own, his regular blog "daveywankenobie" tells the story far better that I can but needless to say that Dave was at the time of our walk, half the man he used to be having lost a shed load of weight already. A coincidence but we passed a makeshift canal side campsite. Is this a better alternative to a shop doorway? I guess this option comes with its own set of problems. Safety in numbers maybe and a chance to stay dry, who knows.....

I have heard a lot about Dave from Julie but this is was the first time we had met. Similar to being on a run, without the face to face contact, walking side by side facilitates open conversation and we shared stories and the journey that brought us together. I shared my stories and the challenges completed and those to come intermingled with those from Dave, we had picked a stunning day to meet and a nice route too with plenty of variety helping to stimulate the discussions not that it needed any help to be honest. Hearing Dave talk so openly about his past and the tough times he had suffered, I realised that the story could have been so different and maybe Dave could have quite easily have ended up on the other side of the counter at the soup kitchen. It's clear that Lady Luck or fate plays a big part in life but also the way you deal with the cards you are dealt can make such a difference to the outcome. We do live in a blame culture and happy to point the finger or deflect blame but sometimes you have to look within for the root cause, then I find you are half way to a solution.

Some interesting items growing on the football pitch as we head back to the car pack, I reckon those mushrooms were magic and with that thought in mind, Dave and I parted but vowed to catch up again. So much more to talk about.....

BACK ON COURT

I would never describe myself as a particularly sporty person, never been into team sports like football, cricket or rugby, school life put pay to that but that another story, but I have always enjoyed racquet sports and back in the eighties when squash became accessible to the masses, me and my mates well and truly jumped on the bandwagon and became obsessed, so when the chance came along to return some thirty years later to the same squash courts that we honed our craft with my lifelong friend Allan was to good an opportunity not to take. I have been friends with Allan since the late seventies, sharing a passion for music, beer and girls along with a desire to save the planet both of us taking to the streets of London with CND back in the Eighties. Sport was more of a distraction to kill time before the pubs opened but today was different, we had the benefit of a proper coach and state of the art racquets, a far cry from the smaller wooden ones and green flash pumps from the old days. With Alison re-educating Al and I in the basics of the game, come on it had been over thirty years, along with actual coaching it was 1983 again. I have known Alison for twenty years, meeting when our kids learnt to swim at the same venue we were at today. LA Fitness back then, Warwick Squash Club before that and today Fitness First and countless names in between.

Both Al and I were amazed how our dormant skills returned and even improved with the just the minimum of coaching, all credit to Alison and her endless patience. I missed the game, the competition and the heathy rivalry lacking from my current sporting activities. Maybe the boys might be back on court again as we did have a great time, but we did respect our advancing years. Some good lessons to take away from this challenge, respect and the ability to adjust what you do but still enjoy the game and most of all, age is just a number, so what did I do with my old racket?

TAKING RESPONSIBILITY

The subject of taking responsibility has cropped up a few times recently, Dave Lancaster and I talked in depth on our recent walk especially in connection with being overweight. I carry an extra pound or two (I can hear your laughing people!) but it's true. I like my food and a beer or two along with no concept of portion control although Julie does try alas in vain I feel, but at no point have I or do I blame anyone. I was a child of the sixties when money was tight, and diets were unheard of. We eat well and very little processed food, that came later, we did eat but no one was counting the calories. We played outside a lot and we definitely lived for the moment and maybe that explains a lot but at no point do I blame my past, the miners' strike, three-day week or Maggie Thatcher. I like to think I take responsibility and that's a life lesson I like to share with my children. My daughter did work at an engineering company close to my heart and at the end of her time, I asked her what she had learnt, "when something goes wrong Dad" she replied, "it's always someone else's fault".

Out of the mouths of babes they say.

We do need to take ownership of our issues and the solution, it is so easy to blame others. Excepting the problem is one that is of our doing really can help the outcome and the future. I have seen that already on this steep learning curve that I am on and charities like Helping Hands who offer a help up for those who have taken the massive step of accepting ownership are the driving force behind my 56notout year. It goes without saying that sometimes the help needs to be a little more simplistic, a hot meal and clean clothes may just be all that is required at that moment. As

Abraham Lincoln said "the best part about life is you get it one day at a time"

I think I was pondering ownership of a hangover in my next blog, or was I?

RUN #24 – MARTI DHESI

Another half full person who lives life like every day could be their last day. A regular dawn runner and dependable, immortalise on the back cover of my "street life" calendar capturing the atmosphere of an early morning outing. I took the photograph with my iPhone during a chilly autumnal run, the trees a golden glow as the leaves prepared to fall marking the arrival of winter. Marti has been a great supporter of many of my wacky ventures so it was good to run with her. Like many of the people I go out with on a regular basis, once we made it a 56notout run, the dynamics changed as did the conversation which was strange and not sure why. The run seemed to have a purpose and as I was getting in to the swing of concept, I made sure early on that we needed to do a short video and pre-warned my runners of the request to write something in my journal giving the opportunity to prepare some words of wisdom. Marti was another friend who is a fusion of Anglo-Indian cultures and if I ever get the chance to go to India, I would be picking this ladies brains without question, it is on the list but there is a big wide world out there and so little time.

RUN #25 – MATT ASQUITH

When the challenge idea was in its early planning stage and I added the plan to run with 56 different people to the list, I had a few runners who I wanted to run with and knew that more people would be added to the list as the year progressed. To run with Matt was a must, I feel like I have known this gent all my life but in reality, it hasn't been that long and I class him as a true friend. He just always seems to be there with support when I really need it and good company too. Matt and I are similar builds, big boned you might say, and both keen cyclists too. I really admire Matt's mindset and view on life. We talked of life, the past, the future, courgettes, runner beans (we both have an allotment) and a plethora of subjects as we ran around Kenilworth early on a Friday morning. Matt is a good person to have around, always happy to help people go the extra mile. Training for a new challenge can be tough on your own but we someone by your side then it's a completely different ball game. We were keen to explore ideas for a 56notout challenge that would involve our running group Zero to Hero, an "on run" brainstorming session throw some good ideas into the pot, hopefully something might bubble to the surface.

Matt would come to my rescue many times as the challenge year progressed.

22nd October 2017 - Reflections

A thought provoking week in the 56notout camp, progress on the challenge list for sure and I feel that I have started to make a little space in my own life.

Meeting some amazing people on this crazy journey is giving me a window on the lives of others and cause and effects of life's many problems and opportunities and how people deal with the situations they find themselves in.

Meeting a kindred spirit and taking time to hear his story opened yet another view of life. The passion for life and change from this guy blew me an away if I am honest, not playing the victim, and taking some ownership for the problem and the solution seems to be a reoccurring theme this week, Did Einstein really define insanity as "doing the same thing repeatedly and expecting different results"? Makes sense to me. Taking some ownership for the problem and not blaming the demons, the government, your parents, the telly etc. and realising that life is far more complicated than that.

Making the time together more poignant was when we passed a small "village" of tents off the beaten track which if now home to some. The need is real, that is becoming clearer with every day of this challenge year, not that it never was really, but seeing it for myself brings it into focus.

I had a great evening last night wallowing in nostalgia rocking out at an ACDC tribute band concert, I woke up the morning with a thick head as I drank a few beers more than was good for me. My fault or shall I blame my buddy for offering to drive…..

Back to the soup kitchen

As the progression of the year brought longer nights and lower temperatures, the 56notout team made a return visit to the Lighthouse for the Monday night soup kitchen. Not a challenge this time but part of the learning journey that the team and I had found ourselves taking. Emma was keen to joined us this time, wanting to see for herself the amazing work going on by our local chosen charity and her account used in my blog tells the story from the heart.

27th October 2017 - A fresh pair of eyes

This week started with another visit to the Helping Hands soup kitchen, this time Emma, who we normally chain to her phone manning the social media, was keen to come along and see where the money is going for herself,

It seemed only right that this week the blog is written by her…

"This week has been a real eye opener for me. On Monday evening I visited the Helping Hands Soup Kitchen. I was anxious beforehand, and I did not know what to expect, or how I would feel – in fact I was quite concerned that I hadn't had my dinner yet and the thought of not eating until 9pm was the cause of a lot of my anxiety. I want to share my experience with all of you for a number of reasons but mainly so that people can realise how big of a problem there is and how easy it is to help those who are helping others.

When we arrived the rest of the volunteers were all ready to go. Straight away one of the lovely ladies said to me "do you want to come on the walk out?" and before I knew it the bags were packed full of hot food, sandwiches, crisps, garlic bread, gingerbread men and lots of other donated goodies and we were on our way out of the door. We walked down the alleyway called "Shaun's Alley" named after someone who was found there overdosed. The volunteer said that she knew just where to go and before we had even walked for 5 minutes we were stopped by a group of homeless men who knew her. I put down my bag of food and before I knew it there were lots of frenzied hands grabbing at the food, asking for "one for their friend", their desperation to eat obvious. They were all so kind and appreciative and thanked us all with such sincerity. I was taken aback by how little food we had left already but we continued our journey down the road stopping as we saw others who needed something to eat. When the bags were almost empty we headed back to the shop. On the way back, the volunteer told me her own story of why she volunteered at the shop. It isn't my story to plaster over Social Media but it made me see that most of the people who help there have all respectively had experiences with homelessness, drugs, mental health issues. How can we get people who haven't been through anything like that to understand how difficult life is for some people and want to be part of the change?

Back at the shop, the queue for food had died down a bit and it felt very calm, although busy, in the dining area. On the menu was some pasta and sauce donated by the Midlands Langar Seva Society, gingerbread men, sausage rolls and donuts donated by Greggs and lots more. I was overwhelmed by the amount of food donated, it brought a tear to my eye in fact, but also realised that although there was a huge amount of food, this may not feed everyone a regular sized portion. As some latecomers arrived and asked for two portions of pasta I did the best I could to divide it up and the young girl I gave it to said "thank you so much, I haven't eaten for four days". Another guy came in when there was no hot food left and someone else who had just received a portion shared half of his with him. It really hit home to me how much we take for granted in everyday life. My anxiety about not eating until 9pm quickly went away.

Sadly, a clean coat, a hot meal and a free haircut doesn't change their situation but the warmth, generosity and kindness of all of the people at Helping Hands and beyond CAN change their situation. They help in so many ways – allowing people to get qualifications, finding them housing, helping them to get jobs, encouraging them to make their lives better themselves.

People are so quick to judge. I've read comments recently on Facebook such as "well we need to get rid of all the crackheads in the City Centre" and "I'm fed up of beggars asking me for money when I'm trying to do my Christmas shopping". Those people you are calling crackheads, beggars... the people who you want to "get rid of" are just that – PEOPLE.

I loved my time at Helping Hands and Lianne and the team are honestly the kindest, most down to earth bunch you will ever meet. All of the people who came in to eat had a different story to tell me, they made me laugh, they made me cry, they made me realise that it doesn't matter who you are, where you come from or where you go to sleep at night – what matters is that you are a decent human being."

PERSEVERANCE, LOGISTICS AND THE POWERS OF PERSUASION

I am not sure where the idea for this challenge came from to be honest, I do know that taking the controls of a digger has been on the list pretty much from the start. I knew the challenge would repeatedly come up against the dreaded issues of health and safety so if I wanted to do it properly and keep myself on the right side of the law I was going to need inside help. When you think of a digger, you think yellow, you think JCB. Go big or go home was a phrase that I like, anyone can settle for average. If I was going to drive a digger, it had to be a big one and I want to do more than just have a play. I knew it would not be easy but I did know someone who might just be able to help. I have known Paul since the late nineties when we worked together on the Jaguar X type launch, on a car that that has long since made its way into the museum ending production some ten years later in 2009, travelling all around Europe together and post Jaguar worked at JCB. Got to be worth the trip surely? So, after many false starts and maybe's the date was in the diary. I had a name and a location but I was a little nervous.

This was something new and I was exposing a layer of my lack of coordination, I knew that driving a digger was going to be a far cry from a family saloon and I might just break something. As I arrived at the quarry, no one had heard of me which is always a good start, but I had a name and in keeping with the spirit of the challenge year, I smiled, I chatted and keeping focused, I would not give in. No one said it would be easy and 80 miles from home, I was not going to give in that easily and turn tails. My patience paid off and after a short wait I was entrusted in the safe hands of Michael Whiston, one of JCB's trainers and as the afternoon unfolded, a top bloke. After the obligatory health and safety briefing, equip with hard hat and a hi-vis vest and was escorted to the quarry. My jaw dropped, I felt tiny and insignificant surrounded by equipment the size of a house, all yellow and all built to do the business. Stepping out of the 4x4, I was handed the keys to a 3CX, I climbed aboard which was a challenge in itself and sat in the drivers seat, the only seat to be honest. The ground looked a long way down and my heart was racing and I hadn't even turned the key yet! Oh my, the unleashed power soon became very apparent, once the pre-flight checks were completed along with a little on the job training and the engine started. The beast was alive and I felt I was perched on top of a wild animal. The power was amazing and as we headed into the heart of the quarry, Mike calmly stood casually in the open doorway looking like he would not be out of place on a moving fairground waltzer and continued to instruct me in quarry etiquette and the ground rules of a digger driver. Driving the 3CX was a strange feeling, the soft tyres gave me the uncertainty of who was actually driving as it wobbled along and headed to the place to do a bit of digging. Spinning around on the seat with the same controls reassigned as if by magic to now control the arm and bucket. I started to take undignified gouges out on the heavy clay earth and was surprised how quickly I seemed to get the hang of it. I had started to relax a little and sensing that I might be getting a little bit cocky, Mike showed be how it was done and effortlessly controlled the bucket still perched in the digger door way. Ok maybe I had a lot to learn. I dug the trenches and then filled them in. The filling in was all about power and without breaking sweat, the earth returned to as we had left it ready for another would be digger driver to go through their paces. Mike's patience was endless and turning around again, it was time to get to grips with the front bucket of this beast. Wow, this was something I would not forget as Mike encouraged me to drive full lick into a small hill and fill my boots!

I soon learnt that you do not stop and ponder life with three tons of Derbyshire's finest earth hovering about your head. I remembered that one and driving into a wall of earth, Mike reminded me that I would break anything, this is what these things do all day long. A great day, taking me way out of my comfort zone and more life lessons.

With power needs to come respect.

Run #26 – Gary Mitchell

I like a run on a Friday afternoon and a run in a place that I drive through twice a day to and from work but have never ran. We met in the chocolate box village of Hampton in Arden, outside the bakers opposite the church 1pm. So close to the second city and Birmingham Airport, Hampton still has the feel of village with its pub, little shop a beautiful church and a bakers of course which I have popped in to occasionally for a Belgium bun or a slab of bread pudding so I did know exactly where to meet. Gary is one of these people who's glass is definitely half full and I love his view of life. Gary was also marathon training and making a much better job than I was.

We explored the village together, stopping outside the stunning Hampton Manor, the former estate of Prime Minister, Sir Robert Peel for our video. The manor its origins traceable back to the Domesday Book, variously passing into the gift of Queen Elizabeth I and Queen Henrietta Maria, wife of King Charles I is full of history and I promise to return to sample the hidden treasures of this magnificent building, Researching for this book, I loved the words from the manors website, *Our house is full of history. Like our food, we honour our classical foundations. Today, we're reimagining our country estate to build a new heritage. Respect for the past, creativity for the now.*

Progress is fine but I like the acknowledgement that not everything needs to be changed for change sake. I see this thread in many aspects of life and just sometimes old equals good.

Like most of us, Gary's life is complicated juggling work/life balance like it seems most of the population but today I felt privileged when Gary let me in to a secret, he was planning to propose to his girlfriend Lucy at the end of the London Marathon, the old romantic. And he did and she said yes and they even made the national press, congratulations both.

Run #27 – Nicola Adams

Nicola was a new face to run with, the introduction came from Helen at Tesco's, one of her colleagues and with the new person came a different location. Yet again, the communication came electronically so was only until the day did I put a face to the name.

The date was agreed, and we planned to meet half way but on the morning of our run, the weather was appalling and with lashing rain. Not what you dream of on a Saturday morning, so I texted Nicola to see if she was a fine weather runner but she didn't miss a beat. "I'm ok if you are" came the reply. We arranged to meet in the middle of nowhere so no risk of mistaken identity. The running gear was a giveaway and I did have my 56notout t shirt on just to be on the safe side. Although the weather was dreadful and the rain lashing down, Nicola's smile was a welcome sight. Leaving the cars, we headed on to the Thwaites Estate. Nicola had a picturesque circular route planned, off the beaten track and affording some stunning views over the rolling Warwickshire countryside and a glimpse of the majestical Chesterton windmill.

Within only a few strides, the rain stopped and I felt like we had known each for years, the conversation flowed and her interest in the challenge and the motivation to take it on was so apparent and for the first time I thought about the impact on others of what I was doing. Nicola wrote in my journal :-

Run with an open heart for today you will make ripples in the huge pond of life, tomorrow you will see what you have achieved.

I knew this would not be the last time Nicola and I would run together and I felt sure that our new found friendship would continue.

4th November 2017 – Opinions

Homelessness seems to be a very emotive subject and it seems opinions are like arseholes, everyone has one.

I can see not everyone can see the need to help others and they think that the situation people find themselves in is either drug fuelled or self-inflicted. For sure this can be the case, but for most, life just has dealt them a bad hand.

When I hear the stories of people who have been helped to get back on course, it gives me a great feeling about the good folks in the world and gives me the strength and determination to continue the challenge.

I remember my mum saying "people in glass houses, shouldn't throw stones" No one's perfect I know but some people who share their opinions, particularly online do make me wonder is they are wired in the same way as me…..

It was a pleasure to meet some great people this week, helping me with some of my tasks and fascinating to hear other people's views on life. In a discussion on a run with one of my new friends, we talked about the ripple effect of the 56notout challenge and the legacy it will leave, never thought of that but can already see that the challenge is doing one of its main objectives – awareness and that has really touched me.

Run #28 – Michaela Townsend

Michaela didn't have any issues with joining me for a run as it did not involve me booking any accommodation. I don't think Michaela will ever leave me in charge of travel arrangements ever again, in fact she hasn't since 2013. I guess you are wondering why? A group of us headed to what felt like the end of the world, Newcastle upon Tyne to take part in the iconic and must do half marathon, the great north run. If you have ever been there you will know exactly what I mean, driving up after work on a Friday night, the journey seemed to last an eternity. But the journey was not the issue, it was where I had arranged for us all to stay. I thought what could go wrong with university halls of residence a stone's throw away from the start. I could not have got it so wrong, the compact and oh so basic accommodation was not to her taste and Michaela has never forgiven me. All that said, the weekend was great, full of highlights too numerous to mention but with all its positives, the rooms at Castle Leazes is the lasting memory and might even have got a mention during today's run.

The summer was well and truly over so today we opted for a Friday afternoon slot in contrast to our usual 5.45am running slot. The run started from my home with the promise of a post run cuppa and a chance for Michaela to have a natter with Julie.

11th November 2017 - Looking ahead

The calm before the storm as they say, a busy week in the 56notout camp with some planning and chasing things up for some of the challenges ahead, but also time take time to reflect.

I do like to stop occasionally (my wife would disagree with me !) and just be with those close to me and ponder life and it meanings, and also plan ahead for the nicer things in life, I do realise that not everyone can look that far ahead. For many the future can be as far away as the next meal or a place to sleep for the night and with the colder weather on its way, I would not want to be outside. However, I always said at the outset, one of my challenges would be to get outside and spend the night and see what it's like to sleep without a roof over my head. I have my sleeping bag and cardboard ready and next Friday is the night, as I join Helping Hands for their annual sleep out in the centre of Leamington, to get what can only be a taste, of what it is really like to spend a night on the streets. I avoided the word sleep there, as I do not expect to get much of that next Friday but I do have the luxury of coming home afterwards to a shower and a hot meal. for that I am grateful. I will let you know how I get on next week...

RUN #29 – IAN BEASLEY

The significance of running with Ian would not become apparent until much later in the year, an introduction to our Zero to Hero running group from Mary Childs, Ian was a fairly new addition to our Sunday gang. On hearing of what I was up to, Ian offered to run with me and as I passed his home twice a day, the logistics of fitting a run in together was pretty straightforward. Ian had a lovely route planned and was delighted that it took in some of my old stomping ground from my youth. Balsall Common had common ground since it was the focus of our social life back in the late seventies and early eighties being a central location for the friendship group to coin a modern phrase although very apt and accurate. On the run I learnt that Ian was a trustee for a Birmingham based charity simply called Helping Birmingham's Homeless and does what it says on the tin and gives front line help for the homeless of the second city, providing food, clothing and essentials to rough sleepers of Birmingham. The charity taking to the streets every Sunday evening to deliver essentials to the coalface, very different to Helping Hands and all about the here and now. Minimal overheads and pretty much a one to one donation vs spend going to feed or clothe someone with an immediate need worrying less about the bigger picture so compliment the work being done by Helping Hands.

It was great to share ideas and thoughts to assist ways in tackling the issues faced by rough sleepers from different angles. The ripples that Nicola talked about starting to show as not long after our run, an impromptu discussion with IAC's charity coordinator John Boyd in the coffee room at the company I work for resulted in a donation to Ian's charity along with a boot full of pot noodles.

Sleep on the streets

From the very first day, when the challenge idea took it's very first breath, the one task I wanted to do was to sleep on the streets. I needed to know, or at least get a flavour of what it's like to be cold, alone and not have a roof over my head. My original plan was to just find a shop door way and take my chance but I was being more than a little naive, I would not have made the morning so common sense prevailed and it was an organised sleep out by Helping Hands to raise awareness and funds that would provide the opportunity to let me experience what it was like to be a rough sleeper. Although I was not alone and support available if required, I still found it tough, my blog gives a raw sense of my night in the cold.

19th November 2017 - Waiting for the dawn.

I like my bed, always have done, but Friday night was different. Leaving home and taking the chilly walk to the centre of Leamington gave me time to think about the night ahead. I could have taken the car rather than walk the couple of miles from home but it didn't feel right to be honest. If I was going to do this, I wanted to do it right. Tonight I was going to take on one of the very first challenges that I scribbled down in my notebook back at the end of 2016 when the idea of the 56 challenge was born. How could I get people on my side and persuade them to part with some hard earned cash? I needed to get at least a flavour of what it's like to spend a night on the streets. As I made my way along the leafy streets of my home town, it felt somehow different and I was apprehensive. Carrying a rucksack and a bit of stubble on my chin, I sensed that people we looking at me different, almost through me. The temperature over the last few days had been dropping so I knew that it was going to be a cold one, but how cold, I would soon find out. Finding my pitch for the night, I built myself a little den out of cardboard and a bit of plastic sheet and then I watched the clock, I watched the band, I wondered around with all I had in a rucksack. That came strange to me, not having a base, somewhere to leave my stuff. I felt very nomadic and lonely. The early evening was OK, listening to the stories of real people who make a difference, the local community copper, a homeless lady and a volunteer who had lost her son to the streets. I checked the time, just after midnight and time try and get some sleep. I had been putting off the inevitable, the time when I had to bed down for the night and see if my shelter would keep me warm.

The streets were noisy; Friday night is party night in most towns. The sirens, the shouting, the general chatter seemed very loud with my head on the ground. I was very uneasy and wanted my own bed but I had a long day ahead of me so needed to at least attempt to get some rest and burying my head in my sleeping bag in an attempt to shut out the world, I managed a few minutes sleep, maybe an hour and then the cold. My cardboard box was going soft, attracting the moisture from the damp grass and the temperature was dropping and I was wide awake. Still noisy and flashing blue lights reflecting of the buildings around me added to the tension. I checked the time, dawn was still hours away and then I needed the loo. Another dimension to the night, I need to leave my warm sleeping back and head off to find the toilet. People were still walking around, groups of people chatted and party goers staggered around in endless circles. They didn't see me, I was invisible and I got the feeling of what the nights are like, only a flavour and I didn't like it. I headed back and attempted to get a little more sleep, not sure I did, but at around 5am, I gave in and sat for an hour and watched the world go by.

I was never so glad to see the dawn…..

This particular challenge really got under my skin, I realised what was important to me and also all the stuff that faded into insignificance once the light faded and the temperature dropped. I was lonely, I was scared and I longed for the dawn of another day. I wondered around, I marked time. I thought, boy did I think. The nights were long at this time of the year but in reality it was not that long but those short hours felt like a life time. I searched inside, for strength and also reflected on my life. I was very aware that this was not real, but on the night of Friday 18th September 2016, it felt real enough.

WHAT'S NEXT ASKED THE MAN?

I have no control over when challenges would happen being at the mercy of event and sometimes venue availability. The idea of a quiz night straight after a sleepless night but there was not much I could do about it. I made a token effort at getting some sleep but with my head buzzing from a night under the stars and the project manager part of my brain looking ahead to the fundraiser planned for the Saturday night. Emma and Bolo had the quiz side of the night all sorted with Julie sorting the raffle prizes, I didn't have a massive amount to do, manly the tech side getting the borrowed sound system to work. I am good at stuff like this having spent many years around bands and theatres.

So here's your starter for ten, no conferring ......

More of a fund raiser than a challenge and a team effort rather than a solo event, I was happy to include the quiz night as one of the 56. The choice of venue was easy to sort, we wanted it local with a stage and cheap drinks. The Nelson Club, just around the corner from home was ideal. The quiz was the first real public event and brought a real eclectic mix of people and a chance to raise the profile of the challenge a little. From the outset, we wanted the quiz night to be special and a little different. I love music and after being let down by a local singer, Aiyana K, a very talented young artist came to our rescue. Her name would test my pronunciation on the night, remember I was sleep deprived but a crib sheet saved the day. I often use the analogy of a swan, graceful on the surface but hiding frantic paddling beneath the surface. I wanted the night to feel relaxed but professional and seamless. The team did me proud, the night was pretty much a sell out with more than a healthy select of local vets to add a bit of competition. We had arranged to get into the hall during the afternoon to set up and allowing the team to transform a traditional working men's club into something special at the cost of less time in bed for yours truly but much better than a last minute panic. Pulling on a favour or two, my long standing keyboard wizard friend Steve Bird provided the PA and my old stash of musical gear provided the rest. It all came flooding back and in a jiffy, we had lights and sound. Aiyana had also agreed to come early to sound check and gave me the first chance to hear her sing "people help the people" originally recorded by Birdie (never heard of him!), the song soon became the soundtrack to the challenge year. I stood on the stage, the room looked amazing. Balloons decorated the tables taking the colour theme from the now familiar logo, red white and green although people might think we had some hidden Italian heritage. Logo printed balloons flanked the stage wings and quiz master Bolo was set up to the side of the stage ready to ask the questions including the one about the name of the dog that found the World Cup (it was Pickles just in case you were interested) and pleased with the progress, we headed out for dinner.

Fed and watered we returned, changed into our 56notout t shirts and awaited the arrival of the contestants. We had a running order but did have the opportunity to ad-lib if required. Which was just as well when one of the great people that have helped us and had planned to thank publicly decided to make an early exit so an impromptu microphone appearance and flowers handed over, but apart from that, the night ran like clockwork and a good time was had by all with some much needed boost to the fund raising pot. Standing in the wings when Aiyana sang the song again and I was in tears.

God knows what is hiding in that weak and drunken heart

I guess you kissed the girls and made them cry
Those hard-faced Queens of misadventure
God knows what is hiding in those weak and sunken eyes
A Fiery throng of muted angels
Giving love and getting nothing back
People help the people
And if your homesick, give me your hand and I'll hold it
People help the people
And nothing will drag you down
Oh and if I had a brain, Oh and if I had a brain
I'd be cold as a stone and rich as the fool
That turned, all those good hearts away

God knows what is hiding, in that world of little consequence
Behind the tears, inside the lies
A thousand slowly dying sunsets
God knows what is hiding in those weak and drunken hearts
I guess the loneliness came knocking
No on needs to be alone, oh save me
People help the people
And if your homesick, give me your hand and I'll hold it
People help the people
Nothing will drag you down
Oh and if I had a brain, Oh and if I had a brain
I'd be cold as a stone and rich as the fool
That turned, all those good hearts away

People help the people
And if your homesick, give me your hand and I'll hold it
People help the people
Nothing will drag you down
Oh and if I had a brain, Oh and if I had a brain
I'd be cold as a stone and rich as the fool
That turned, all those good hearts away

I think the song resonated with others too looking at the faces of her audience. One very talented lady and I hoped that we would be able to hear Aiyana sing again, hold that thought.

With a successful night behind us, we headed home to a warm bed with clean sheets, a distant cry from the previous night.

It probably goes without saying that I slept like a baby.

STREET LIFE PHOTO CHALLENGE

I really enjoyed this challenge and better for being given to me by my great friend and running buddy, Sue Cox. I was to provide photographs capturing the life of the streets which would be used for a calendar for me to sell to raise money for the two charities. In the week run up to the quiz night, the aptly named Street life calendar was finished and using the first off samples, the local paper had agreed to help us go public and the showroom at the printers became a makeshift photographer's studio and plunged Sue Cox, my super talented graphic artist and Stuart Crowley, who does all the clever stuff getting design to paper, reluctantly into the spotlight.

I have really enjoyed this particular challenge, the brief was to capture street life, twelve photographs plus one for the cover and maybe one for the back-depicting street life, as simple as that. I thought that too. I provided the photographs and Sue would do the artwork and Stuart and the gang from ARM would do the printing. I gathered images as I went along, the first one I took ended up on the cover, the picture of a broken umbrella on a rainy street. This was taken during an early morning run and set the feel of the calendar. I also wanted to have pictures to capture the ever changing seasons and traditions of this great country of ours but there was one image that I wanted to use, that of my late father in law who died early in the challenge year and thought fitting that Ron was remembered. The photo captured Ron "blending" in with locals in a street cafe in his favourite city, Paris and won me second prize in the local agricultural show. "An

Englishman in Paris", a black and white image dedicated to the great man was a fitting tribute to a lovely gentleman.

Having created a potential folder ready to shortlist for the final product, I knew I would have too many, but I had some that I really wanted to use. I knew enlisting a second opinion was fraught with danger but understanding the risks, I went through my final selection with Julie, the obvious choice of critic as I wanted to use one of her photographs. I had tried to capture the same image, fish and chips on the seafront, but her picture had the edge over mine so giving her the credit, this was a great shot for a summer month. Other selections took a little more discussion but finally we had the photographs, all except a photograph for the final month. It had to be winter/Christmas or something along those lines and pretty to the wire, with Leamington Christmas light switch on providing the December image and with that, we had product.

A spontaneous photograph taken on a dawn run which provided the atmospheric back drop to the calendar story for the back-cover immortalising Marti Dhesi, runner #24 during a winter run. Just in time for Christmas, the sales drive started and by the end of year, the stocks were gone and happy to see calendars travelling to North America, Germany and Sweden and the UK of course along with pretty much every desk in my office. The support was overwhelming and nice to have a product to sell rather than asking for a handout. A great challenge and adding a lovely surge of cash into the pot.

A bonus that came to the surface sometime after the challenge year was over and brought a smile to my face and a warm glow to my heart. My eldest daughter, Libby, a newly qualified secondary English teacher did not want to throw her calendar away at year end so she cut it up keeping the photographs and used them as visual aids for constructive writing - nice. I do like a bit of recycling and reading the words that the pictures provoked in others was brilliant.

PERCEPTION

Having had some issues of the original challenge regarding haircuts and facial hair which I had to adapt the idea. I planned to go 56 days without a haircut or shaving, but reactions did surprise me enough to adjust the challenge to just growing a beard. You would have thought this challenge would have been easy but I never been follicularly challenged and whenever I have tried to grow a beard it has never gone well. I tried back in the eighties with limited success but thankfully the result had to be removed with imminent best man duties which demanded a clean shaven image from the grooms mum and again a few years ago which unfortunately resulted in a snow white and a little patchy excuse for a beard adding 10 years to my already advancing years but I wanted to see the impact on people with a change of my appearance, would I be treated differently.

I let my hair grow and left the razor in the bathroom cabinet, but it didn't take long before the world started to notice. I started to look scruffy and soon my boss noticed, and I could see his point, I was not customer facing but I do have to deal with all the spectrum of people within the organisation up to the Vice President and appearance does mater.

Longer hair and a little facial hair do not change my ability to do my job one little bit but as for perception, that's a completely different kettle of fish and I soon realised that maybe a haircut would be in order along with a shave.

I had proved my point but wanted a photo for my blog, but the mass of grey hair did not want to appear on the photograph so time for the addition of a little mascara to make the beard stand out a little. I wanted the photo to prove a point so I shaved half my face. Unfortunately I did look like a serial killer but the challenge had done its job. Image is everything and perception is better than fact, it soon made me realise.

Needless to say, my boss was pleased to see the return of a clean shaven member to his team. It did make me realise that appearance, especially first impressions really do matter.

RUN #30 – DAVE DAW

No trip to Warwick is complete without bumping into Dave, usually when I have a beer in my hand or walking out the chippy with a bag of brown food so today was good as we had arrange to meet so I didn't need to hide. Dave is another of my fellow runners that I had known for a while but didn't actually know much about. A friend of a friend who I didn't realise actual lives just around the corner, so to run just the two of us was not only easy but different with the absence of others. I learnt about Dave's past, his roots and what brought him to the town that we are very happy to call home. We both like people and a solitary lifestyle would suit neither of us, so no surprises that we always bump in to each other in the thick of the action.

25th November 2017 - Catching my breath

A pretty manic week in the 56notout camp, having barely recovered from the sleepout, the team and I were straight into the quiz. The feedback has been great and added another £840 to the pot with talented Aiyana K's moving performance of People help the People and words from Paddy and Leanne from Helping Hands providing a poignant back drop to a brilliant night.

With barely time to catch our breath, the last photo and final tweaks to the 56notout calendar. A challenge set by Susan Cox, to capture "Street life" and sell the calendars to raise awareness and more money, just like being on The Apprentice – thank you for the opportunity! A round of photo shoots, newspaper appearances and a radio interview with Lorna Bailey of BBC CWR added to an already busy week along with a run or two.

Looks like winter is on its way and maybe some snow! Be afraid… running naked in the snow is still on the list.

I am nearly halfway so thought it was time to give you the "scores on the doors" so far.

Challenges completed – 20 (36 to go)

Challenges started – 2 with plenty in the diary.

Money raised £2055 to date

Thank you to everyone who is following, helping, donating – it's really is appreciated.

RUN #31 — ALI DAVIS

I have Facebook group "Running the World" to thank for meeting Ali, the social media running community does exactly what it says on the tin bringing runners together from all over the world. I love reading posts from fellow runners in every corner of the globe and the exciting and very different places they run and some of the unusual things they met on route. Reading each other's offerings online, it was obvious we lived near each other, the photographs of Warwick Castle one of the biggest giveaways.

I invited Ali to join our little running club, but she seemed reluctant about coming along on my repeated offers to have a Sunday run. "I am not great with big groups of new people" came the reply, so wanting to extend the hand of friendship, I agreed to meet her ahead of meeting the group so we could get to know each other a little before exposing her to the rest of the gang. Ali and I hit it off straight away, once she realised that I was not a serial killer.

A shy and cautious individual with a passion for running who as I have learned over the years, has not had the easiest of lives. Running is clearly Ali's escape, a chance to put on the trainers, don the headphones and just be herself. We talked about past events, the first time we ran together was the 2015 Birmingham Half Marathon when she joined Libby and I for the annual 13.1 miles trot around the second city.

The three of us stayed together pretty much all the way around and we had a ball, it didn't feel like exercise at all as we lapped up the support from the crowd lining the route. Ali posed the question as to what I had planned once the challenge year was over. I had started to give the subject some thought and I had already decided to ease off on the running and planned not to enter any events for at least a year along with generally easing off everything whilst A) I wrote this book, B) allowed my body to recover and C) finished all the stuff that I had not done in the last 12 months.

Every time we meet, Ali does ask me what races have I got booked, the same answer - nothing!

RUN #32 – JEZ HOWELLS

Jez is a fun guy, always good to chat with and never fails to bring a smile to my face. A true people person and very much with a half full glass. I am not sure how I got to know Jez and his lovely wife Linda and his extended family apart from they have all ran with our little group from time to time, generally adding a new dimension to the conversation. Whether it's dogging, how we got on that subject, God only knows or the lack of knowledge that the Krankies were actually husband and wife, Jez thought that they were both blokes, you can always count on a memorable tale or two. I have not had a proper chat with Jez for a while as he is always either playing golf, on holiday or on a golfing holiday so was good to have a catch up.

Jez is a little like me in as much as he likes the people side of running rather than the running so we focused on life and less about the running, so we were both happy. I like people that you don't see all the time but when you do, you just carry on from where you left off, effortless conversation. As with many of my 56notout running companions, it seems that the busy people can always find some time to help others. Jez has got a good handle on work/life balance and as soon as the better weather comes, the Howells family hitch up the caravan and head to somewhere new to spend some quality time away from the hamster wheel. I need to get some tips but do not fancy a caravan.

One day more

I'm not shy, I get around - to quote a line from the eighties rock band Foreigner, classic tune, "Urgent", but to walk out on stage in front of 1300 people at Warwick Art Centre would push me way out of my comfort zone but before I could tick off another challenge first I had to get a solo and that would mean going for an audition. I needed help to pull this off and Julie was up for being my side kick. Barry Todd, musical director of Midland Voices had planned a couple of classic songs from *Les Misérables* in the December show and the part of the *Thénardiers,* the duplicitous innkeepers, had our name written all over it. The rough and ready inn keeper and his wife was perfect for us. When Julie suggested we practiced I was not so keen, I am a bit of a "just do it" sort of person and much preferred to just wing it. Walking into the rehearsal room for a run through before heading in to audition, I started to panic, maybe we should have practiced a little bit more but it might be a little late now. We will be fine I told myself, smile and wave and act confident I told my inner self. We can do this and we did, I liked to think Barry, Carol and Chris saw potential in our short but convincing rendition of "one day more" and a few days later we had the email, we had done it. A few extra lines to learn, costumes to sort and more rehearsals. I can sing in a group but a solo would strip away the layers and expose my weaknesses. I did have Julie by my side and a few months to practice.

A bonus of having a solo was the chance to go to the band call, the orchestra's rehearsal and of course then need to hear where the choir fit in to the score so not only do we get chance to listen to this talented group of musicians practice, we get chance to sing the complete show along with our own solos of course but also to hear in a intimate setting, all the sounds and textures of the orchestra, just an amazing experience.

The toughest part of having a solo, I soon learnt, was performing in front of the rest of the choir, a very critical audience. Having done that a couple of times, the show would be a breeze - time will tell.

As we were singing as part of a set piece, costumes were required. Julie had it covered and a trip to our local party store and we soon looked the part. Unscrupulous inn keeper and his misses, the part could have been written for us and a chance to ham it up a little. No one would see anyone's outfit until the day and a photo call backstage provided a great memory of the challenge. Our little chance of fame was to end the main part of the show and Barry thought that to save a lot of movement, we could stay on stage for the encore. With any performance, timing is everything.

We practiced our walk on, to get eight of us on stage from both sides of the stage needed to look right, professional. Standing backstage waiting for our cue, I felt unbelievably calm.

We were ready, walking out, with the woman I love, I felt great. The audience seemed close, I could see the faces. Let's do this. As long standing friend Bob Hoskins sang the open lines "One day more, another day another destiny ...." and before we knew it, it was all over and we were taking our bows. I loved it and glad that I was not on my own to share this wonderful experience and one I never thought I had the balls to do.

As One Day More was the final song of the main show, we stayed on stage for the inevitable encore. At the front, with the orchestra and all choir behind us, we sang our hearts out for the last number, one of my favourite songs, the incredible Anthem with rousing and uplifting music by Benny Andersson and Björn Ulvaeus of the ABBA together with thought provoking lyrics by Tim Rice, from the musical Chess.

One amazing day and what a way to end it, I might just have shed a tear or two such is the power of music.

10th December 2017 - Tis the season!

I am looking at Christmas in a different way this year for a number of reasons, when I think about what we perceive as important at this time of year, the countdown to Christmas, who will win the X factor and which department store has the best TV ad, I realise that it doesn't really matter a month , when the future is as far away as tomorrow for some people , it puts life in perspective and you see what is really important.

I had the pleasure to see our youngest grandson perform in the school nativity this week, the messages rang out loud and clear as to what was really important. We are not all the same and to be different is ok, these little ones did not pre judge or worry about what they each had or didn't have, or the colour of their skin. These children will learn that later from the grown-ups, along with the belief that we have to have it all, peer pressure and society as whole. Sometimes we need to spend a little time in the "playground" a get back to basics to find out what really matters.

With the arrival of winter in the past few weeks, I needed a hat and gloves to keep out the cold and rummaging in my drawers, I found I had about 6 pairs of gloves and as many hats pretty much all the same. How many hats is enough? I think it's time to de-clutter and the run up to Christmas and the year end is always a good time to do a stock take on your life. We only need what's enough and others have nothing, so maybe now is a good time to address the balance a little and I know the local and national charities welcome items of warm clothing and sleeping bags as the temperatures plummet and can get your goodies to the right people. Seeing the incredible number of shoe boxes filled with treats and Christmas cheer being handed out by Helping Hands to the families in need along with toys for the Children, makes me realise that the world is not such a bad place after all and there is a glimmer of hope for this crazy world of ours.

RUN NAKED IN THE SNOW

Snow is a bit like sex, you never know how many inches you are going to get and how long will it last.

Running naked in the snow was one of the first challenges I scribbled on the list over a year ago. We rarely get snow and it did make a good conversation piece, generally to raised eyebrows. I was always vague about the detail of the challenge, location etc., as I didn't really want to be arrested for public indecency as going to prison was never a challenge. Snow had be threatened for days so when I looked out of the window to a good couple of inches of snow I was not surprised. My phone had already made incoming text noises, knowing that others would have seen the snow too. Some very subtle messages, "Steve, it's snowing ......!" "You said!?" Ok I get the message. I had the idea but lacked a robust plan, so I thought sod it, trainers on, grabbed my camera (I need the evidence of course) and Julie, to take the photos and cover my arse so to speak.

As soon as I left the house, Julie immediately pointed out that I have a family, daughters to be accurate and this would have to be filmed sympathetically if it was going to end up on social media to save embarrassment. Heading out of the front door in just a pair of trainers was a surreal experience but quite liberating if I am honest.

It was light but I seemed to be the only early bird this morning so I went for it and ran down my road with Julie capturing the image of my bare backside running of into the distance for posterity, unfortunately and not for the camera, she had to see my return journey which was not a pretty sight. The cold air on my skin was lovely and surprisingly I did not feel uncomfortable but thinking that I had maybe pushed my luck a little, we headed back inside. Before the image appeared on social media, my white buttocks had acquired a logo to save embarrassment however some select folks have seen the unedited version and for this I am truly sorry.

I was hoping that this might have got me some national publicity but alas, I was upstaged by Oli Murs in a bloody Christmas jumper!

17th December 2017 - A mad flourish….

The arrival of snow did bring home to a lot of people including me that although it can be great fun to play in, it is not the best conditions to live out in. With snow days a plenty for schools, life carries on but getting around in these icy conditions is not the easiest. I for one would not want to be on the streets at any time of the year but -10'C! the way those who care stepped up to the plate, people helping people, filled me with hope. The spirit is alive I feel, but some adverts on TV do make me wonder when it seems Christmas is all about the size of the telly for some. Maybe we need to look a little deeper sometimes. To those people and organisations who have opened their doors and hearts to help, you are the best!

On a positive side for the 56notout team, I am ticking a few more challenges off with another flourish promised before the end of 2017, so I feel that the New Year can start on a positive note. The sale of calendars is going well and still have a few left if anyone would like one, £7 each, the price of a couple of coffees.

Excitement in the camp too with a new challenge on the cards for the Spring and the opportunity to learn more about one of the lesser known causes of homelessness and the impact on those who some see as different. Although we are not all the same, a boring world if we were, acceptance and understanding of different lifestyles can be hard for some and the result can be prejudice and ignorance.

More about this and other challenges after the holidays there may be some that you want to get involved with and challenge yourself too while having a bit of fun….

But for now, the lycra is back on to attempt something I never thought I would do and it's nothing to do with running .... All will be revealed, although you will be glad to hear, not as much as last week!!

YOU WANT ME TO DO WHAT?

Many challenges were on the original list and others evolved from ideas or conversation, but the next challenge came out of the blue and was a cracker. I have zero flexibility, weigh the wrong side of 16 stone and lack any sense of balance so when Michelle Dunn invited me to try my hand at acro yoga, I knew this was going to test me. I knew as soon as arrived at the studio I was way out of my depth. The welcome committee of slim, fit smiling ladies who collectively weighed in less than me should have rang the warning bells, I was a little concerned that I was about to make a fool of myself. The assembled experts including Michelle along with leader Jenni made me so at ease I soon started to look forward to trying something different.

Flexibility was my biggest worry and I found even the warm up exercises more than a little taxing but faint heart never one fair maiden and before long I was on the floor and providing a slightly larger than normal "base" for these amazingly agile ladies and even got chance to "fly", the technical term for being held in the air but with the lack of any charm or grace.

After making a video log with a vailed attempt at humour and watching in absolute admiration as to how it should be done, I returned home for a soak in the bath and a cuppa, delighted to have tried something different and ticked another challenge off the list.

24th December 2017 - Christmas Eve

A bit of a Christmas tradition in the Atherton household and many others I suspect is watching one of the iconic Christmas Films – Love Actually. The opening lines of the film really made me think....

"Whenever I get gloomy with the state of the world, I think about the arrivals gate at Heathrow Airport. General opinions starting to make out that we live in a world of hatred and greed, but I don't see that. It seems to me that love is everywhere. Often, it's not particularly dignified or newsworthy, but it's always there - fathers and sons, mothers and daughters, husbands and wives, boyfriends, girlfriends, old friends. When the planes hit the Twin Towers, as far as I know, none of the phone calls from the people on board were messages of hate or revenge - they were all messages of love. If you look for it, I've got a sneaky feeling you'll find that love actually is all around."

I promise I will not burst in to song but seeing the great things going on in the last few weeks has made me realise that the world is full of great people doing some amazing things and helping others to find a better future or just make today just that little bit better.

Homelessness seems to be in the news a lot these days and the issues facing the people without a place to call home on the increase. It's good that the problems are coming to the top of the list for discussion and resolutions too by those who can make a difference and listening to MP's talking about the lack of social housing and the need to build more isn't rocket science and just maybe the solution can be found by looking back in history. Without trying to get political, was homelessness as much of an issue back in the sixties when we had council houses? I will leave you with that thought...

From the 56notout team, we with you a Merry Christmas and take care X

Run #33 – Harkx Kalsi

Boxing Day and the second run with Harkey in as many days, we ran together yesterday, yes Christmas Day taking part in the annual trot around Saint Nicholas Park. To be honest, I usually run on Christmas morning with my eldest daughter Libby but this year we all decided to mix it all up a bit and all stay local so I thought I'd take a break from tradition and stay in my PJ's for a change but Julie, my other half did not think much to the idea of having me in the house all day with pent up energy and found me a local run to take part in. The annual Christmas Day run organised by Leamington AC and Kenilworth Runners, the event now in its 47th year was a good excuse to blow way the cobwebs. It was like a home from home with many fellow runners having the same idea. I did run with Harkey but didn't feel right having another 60 plus other runners with us to talk turkey so we planned to meet the following day.

I love running with Harkey, this girl just ouses enthusiasm with a real passion for life and an amazing artist/graphic designer. We talked of life changing decisions and sometimes you have to take a leap of faith if you want something to happen. A quote that I really like (frequently attributed to Albert Einstein, Benjamin Franklin, or a number of other people who probably never said it) is that insanity may be defined as "doing the same thing over and over and expecting different results." But is true, if you want to make a change to your life that you must do something different. Harkey did just that, packing up her metaphorical spotted hanky and head off to London to find her fame and fortune.

I know from experience that this is not that easy to leave home and throw caution to the wind so we both have this in common. Still early days for my young friend but she can already claim to have a piece of her work on the wall of the famous Richard Branson. I think the future is looking good for my festive running buddy. If my other book ever sees the light of day then I am sure Harkey's artwork will adorn the cover as it perfect for the subject.

He's behind you!

You knew that was coming I am sure. Time has always been an issue so when the challenge to appear in a traditional pantomime was added to the list I knew the task had to be a one night only type deal with little or no prep. If I was going to do this, then I wanted a big audience. Cinderella at the Belgrade theatre in Coventry fitted the bill. So part of the challenge year was to use a number of life skills, negotiation, persuasion and charm, all these came into play to make this happen. The team at the theatre were brilliant and no sooner than I made the initial contact on the phone the progress was very impressive. I learnt very early on that actually speaking to someone on the phone was the best way to get results. Emails can get lost in the ether and can be a little impersonal - it's always good to talk. Little did I know is that the team had the same idea so once the common request found the same person the deal was done, and I would be taking to the stage.

We have a family tradition of a trip to the panto, pretty much the full family, daughters, stepdaughters, partners, husbands and grandchildren of course. Having let Steve Cressy, the stage manager at the theatre, know where we were sitting (we did have to make a swift move of seats as we were originally in the circle and to make this work, we had to be in the stalls to get on the stage) I kept quiet so the family were not aware. Steve, let me know the rough idea of the plan and that I would not be in my seat much.

Typical on the day, I didn't feel great with the early signs of the flu but the show must go on. Taking to our seats, I am waiting in anticipation as the lights went down - show time. I wondered how long it would be before the fun started. I had an idea of the plot, so I soon started to see the signs and sure enough I was on stage as one of the ugly sisters' boyfriends. I was a willing victim but the other chap, had been nominated as a possible candidate for public humiliation. My "partner" was panto legend Iain Lauchlan who was brilliant, I love panto, English eccentricity at its finest.

I am sure I spent longer on the stage than in my seat enjoying having a chat with the other boyfriend in the interval, both of us enjoying the limelight to be honest and I enjoyed the chance to do my sales pitch and worked as people gave me donations at the interval. Steve was on hand to take photographs and the family were thrilled when Iain invited us back stage at the end of the show, seeing our granddaughter, Grace's face as she posed for photos in Cinderella's carriage was a picture and going backstage gave me a chance to thank Steve in person.

An amazing night for the team.

Run #34 – Becci Heath

With snow on the ground but this time fully dressed, the days between Christmas and New Year provided a perfect opportunity to catch up with busy mum and good friend Becci Heath who also works in the car industry so benefits from a decent break over the Christmas period. We picked an absolutely stunning day to put our trainers on, glorious sunshine, blue skies and firm ground. Becci has a pre-school daughter so was recovering from a pretty full on run up to holidays plus the big day itself so a chance to blow the cobwebs away did us both good. The cross-country run afforded the chance to approach Kenilworth Castle from the west, without question the most photogenic view of the magnificent ruins.

The covering of snow added to the atmosphere and made the Warwickshire countryside look just the best. Although freezing cold, the bright winter sun testing the camera on my smartphone and my selfie skills but help was at hand in the guise of a passing walker. A great way to enjoy a beautiful day and best of all, no work today as the holidays continue,

30th December 2017 - Looking back, looking forward.

Bad weather, illness and just life in general has had its impact on the progress of challenges lately but still heading in the right direction and still enjoying the journey. Only five months to go now and there is still plenty on the list, so if you have offered to help with a challenge or two, or fancy joining me for a run then I will be coming after to you!

The support has always amazed me and has restored my faith in human nature, on a recent challenge, to appear in panto I was overwhelmed by people. With the help of Steve, Iain and the crew of the

Belgrade Theatre in Coventry, I managed to tick another challenge off the list. strangers giving me money for the cause was worth the public humiliation but what also brought a tear to my eye was hearing that the theatre was also spreading the festive cheer by giving away over 600 tickets for its pantomime Cinderella to local families in need as part of its Making Memories campaign, there are some great people out there ...

Scores on the doors
Challenges completed – 24 (32 remaining)
Challenges started – 2 with another 20 or so in planning stage.
Money raised £2125.66 so far with another £300 or so to be added from the sale of the calendars.

Thank you to everyone who is following, helping, donating and supporting us

Looking forward now to a productive 2018 and even the dreaded Marathon training,

Wishing you a Happy New year....

Just in case you have any money left after Christmas and sales......

WELCOME TO 2018 – NIGEL RUSSELL #35

As 2017 turned into 2018, I did feel the pressure come on, I was a far cry from where I wanted to be with the number of months remaining you could count on one hand. Taking a few weeks out had left its mark on challenge progress with the exception of running with 56 different people which was well on plan. When I started this challenge, I thought I would run with many people I have ran with before but already I had the opportunity to run with some lovely new people along with old friends too, but even with these people, the dynamics was completely different. Plenty to talk about for sure but also interesting to hear others view on what I was doing and their thoughts of the problems fancy those on the streets of our towns and cities. I love people and happy to listen as well as talk when spending time on a run. Rarely running in silence, conversation comes easily find the lives of others really interesting and can see how busy folks these days are and when out in the trainers, an opportunity to enjoy some quality time with someone.

Helen, my new friend and great supporter of local charities including Helping Hands introduced me to another new person to run with, Nigel Russell and somewhere different too. After swopping a message or two, I headed to meet Nigel at his house in Napton.

I am generally comfortable meeting new people and just get on with it, rarely struggle to find something to talk about and a common interest or two. Today's running companion was a pleasure, conversation flowed complimented by a lovely route showcasing Warwickshire at its best. I felt a real connection with Nigel, I loved hearing about his life and family and great things that he had planned plus we were of a similar running ability which made it a pleasure. Returning back to "his" to meet his wife, Sheral and their grandchildren was a bonus, coffee and biscuits too, rude not to.

6th January 2018 - Turning the page

Happy New Year!

With less than 5 months of the challenge left, I can see the pressure starting to build a little and will be happy when I start to tick a few more off the list. With the start of a new year comes a lot of resolutions for many and some even make it to the second week. Have you made any? I like the start of a new year as I see it as a chance to draw a line and start afresh and recalibrate life a little. With the London Marathon only 16 weeks away, I have started eating better hoping to shed a pound or two to make the 26.2 miles a little easier on the knees and keeping away from alcohol during the week, "Dry January" was a bit of an ask but I do have another challenge lined up for next month that will hopefully help my waistline and swell the pot too, as I attempt 56 days alcohol free, with day 57 the day of the marathon. I will need a drink after that for sure!

Over the holiday, preoccupied with the usual Christmas and New Year distractions, I did stop to think about those people who did not give a fig about resolutions and dry January having far more important things to worry about, like the next meal or hoping that the weather doesn't get any colder. What do people on the streets do when they are ill?

The plight of the homeless and those who are doing so much to help them are making headlines recently, I don't remember seeing anything like this level of homelessness when I was a kid, but didn't we have council or social housing back then? I am not politically motivated, but I cannot help thinking that the some of the solutions could lie in the past, not all progress is beneficial – I will leave that thought with you.....

Look back to move forward

As the challenge year progresses, the problems that face the world today is really starting to get under my skin. Many of the issues in today's society are nothing new but with progress and evolution maybe some are. Are a lot of the issues facing many of us today of our own doing, as we all strive for the best, the bigger, the latest? Thought provoking and maybe a controversial point of view, but the year has made me look at myself and my life. As for the problems, maybe some of the answers can be found in the past.

Not all progress is good, looking back at my own childhood when a large proportion of my school friends, like me, lived in a council house, most people did, We still experienced the extremes of society, the haves and the have nots but I don't recall food banks, rough sleepers and the scale of homeless that we see on the streets of our towns and cities that we do today. Are council houses, or social housing the answer? Maybe it is but don't sell the bloody things off with a change of government and a fresh pair of eyes. The people we pay to run this great country of ours should look back in to the past where the answer to the today's issues could be found which might just make for a better future, just a thought....

Saturday 13th January 2018 - Turning up the pressure

Today was different for me and special to have a run with runner number 36, my 10-year-old grandson, and it was lovely to spend some time with him, although he left me standing with very little effort! Age is

177

no qualification and Jack is very aware of the world around him and is very caring. Children are the future (I thought it was garlic bread , sorry couldn't resist a Peter Kay joke..) and hearing about the effort going in at schools to break the cycle of poverty, to educate and help families to get a route to a better life was interesting, as behaviour breeds behaviour. People say the apple doesn't fall far from the tree but if that was really true, we would still be living in caves. People can change but sometimes they just need someone to listen to them and a helping hand.

Having given myself a week to settle into the routine, I have now started upping the pressure to get as many challenges in the diary as I can so I do not run out of time, so be prepared for a message or two if you have offered to help.

I am really looking forward to Alton Towers; I do love a roller coaster. NOT !!, never been a big fan of fairs or theme parks so this really is a challenge, and way out of my comfort zone. I cannot help thinking that some other challenges might be heading my way that I might not be so keen on but I can't enjoy myself to much can I? At least I still have plenty of people lined up to run with, fancy joining me? Drop me a message and we can get something in the diary. I am still waiting for Daniel Craig to get back to me.....

Out of the mouth of babes

Putting on my trainers to run with my grandson Jack McGinty was very special, 10 years old and the youngest person that I had the pleasure to run with. Jack was very aware of life and those who are not a fortunate as him, a very caring young man. We talked of life and the future, very grown up stuff for someone of tender years. I love hearing about his hopes and dreams but was lovely to look back to the past and reminisce on the fun times that we have had. Cooking sausages on the beach at Wonwell, during a family holiday was one of our lasting memories that we have shared together and such a great memory. A perfect night, a stunning location - flying kites, paddling in the water and sausages cooked on a BBQ along with a glass of wine or two, I can see Jack doing this with his kids but alas I might not be around to see it and does put me in touch with my immortality. Jack was the first of three Grandchildren and hope that more will come along before I exit this planet. We ran along the river and into the park, oh to be young again, Jack never broke sweat but I can be forgiven that I was a little moist as I do have 45 plus years on him, a lifetime. As we ran, we chatted and loved hearing his thoughts on life. Out of the mouth of babes as they say. The now infamous video took a bit of doing, we talked through the process but even with all the planning, it did take a few takes to get it sorted and provided one of the funniest memories of the challenge year, but we got there eventually. Photos and videos done, we headed for home, but Jack still had an abundance of energy so whist I headed back for a cuppa, joined his brother and sister for a visit to the swing park with their dad. After a bit of fun in the park, the crew returned home, and Jack wrote a short but lovely entry in my journal.

"Really enjoyed my run with Grandpa Steve and so happy to be part of challenge 56notout -Jack."

Brought a tear to my eye, Jack is the future and I'm proud to be part of his present.

To be the eyes of another

Ellen had been a great supporter from our meet in the ketchup outfit earlier in the year and had helped me with one the most memorable challenges when she had arrange me to run without sight back in the autumn and I wanted to see if I had what it takes to be the eyes of another, it's a trust thing. I have met Maggie a few times, but would she put her trust in me and let me guide her on a training run ahead of her next event - the Milton Keyes half marathon and was keen to up the miles.

Meeting in Kenilworth, Ellen already had a route in mind and soon we were on our way. Once we had crossed the road and on to a car free track, Ellen handed over control, phew no pressure but Ellen assured me that Maggie would teach me on the job and I really appreciated her instant trust in. Happy that I was in doing ok and Maggie seemed at ease, the conversation started to flow, and we all got to know each other. We talked openly as if we had known each other all our lives, punctuating the conversations with the odd instruction or description of the route for Maggie. As we headed out into the countryside, I was unaware of what was to come, up to now, I was linked to Maggie by a short cord, but Ellen was about to bring me tears.

Pointing out that a straight clear path lie ahead, no people, dogs or anything that could trip her, Maggie knew what was coming. "Let go of the cord Steve, let Maggie run on her own". The look of freedom on Maggie's face was a delight to see and her beaming smile infectious, the tears rolled down my cheeks. A special afternoon and a privilege to spend with two amazing people, they had extra miles to run so turning for home, I pondered the time together and treasured a wonderful challenge.

Ellen wrote a lovely piece in my journal and was lovely to read her take on the afternoon: -

"Maggie and I first met Steve at the start of the two castles run, obviously he was dressed as a bottle of tomato sauce. Being Maggie's guide, I try and describe as much as possible so she can soak up pre-race atmosphere to the max. Describing Steve's outfit to a lady who had been blind from birth was too much of a challenge so we went for a feel! It turns out Steve had heard about us two and been meaning to get in touch with us so we could all run together. So began the back and forth of trying to fix a date!

Now so Steve knew what he was getting himself into he came along to Stratford upon Avon parkrun first- to be blindfolded. I had organised, what turned out to be his friend, to guide him blindfolded around our course so he could get a little appreciation of what it's like to run without being able to see. He did really well, 35:49! So he was ready......

Eventually Steve joined us on one of Maggie's training runs for the Milton Keynes marathon. Maggie and I had to do 9 miles and Steve ran with us for 6 of them. We were running on the Kenilworth Greenway which was a perfect place for Steve to guide Maggie for the first time- he wanted a challenge! Well he took to it like a duck to water or tomato sauce to chips?! What amazed me is how much talking he could still do 'while guiding, I think it was an art!! It was such a happy chirpy run listening to all of Steve's' adventures what an inspirational man.

Maggie doesn't have easy access to Facebook, where I watch Steve's challenges unfold, so when we run together, I update her on his latest challenge. Our last run we talked about how on earth he ran the London marathon in the heat in his ketchup bottle.

It was a real pleasure for us to run with Steve and to offer a bit of support for his 56 Not Out challenges. Best of luck Steve and if you ever want to guide again then shout!

Time for bigger balls

I often ponder how much longer I can keep running for as I am not getting any younger and my body, especially my joints starting to give me more than the occasional aches and pains, I suspect it will not be much longer so when I was challenged to try a new sport, I jumped at the chance to give it a go as long as it didn't involve heights or water or even worse, heights and water, don't worry Tom Daley, the thought of jumping off a diving board breaks me in to a cold sweat just thinking about it. I have heard of racket ball, often called old man's squash so was off to a good start already and but knew nothing about it apart from the fact it's a bit like squash, but you need bigger balls!

My old buddy Allan, who is a year or two older than me is already showing signs of wear and tear ending his running activities although he is still partial to the gym and as competitive as ever, we both could do with a new sport. Arriving to Fitness First for the second time in the challenge year meeting now Racquetball coach Alison, swoping hats from Squash Coach in a previous challenge, we returned to court but this time with a racket the size of a car and a ball the size of a small dog, ok I might have got my scales a little wrong but bigger than squash equipment so we were in with a chance of hitting the ball a little more often. A couple of bodily ailments do hinder any sport involving movement and hand/eye coordination - flexibility, I am like a board and eyesight, my mum was right..... I need glasses to see pretty much anything these days, but I relied on the force rather than vision for today's challenge. Under the expert guidance of Alison, Al and I were soon playing the game, old man's squash seeing fitting, and both really enjoyed this new experience proving you can teach an old dog new tricks.

Sitting outside the court, post-game we both remarked that this might just be the sport for us.

Saturday 20th January 2018 - Trust me!

A busy week in the 56notout camp with lots of calls and emails to get as many challenges in the diary in the next few weeks so I can plan the remainder of the time left, I would like to sleep in May so any help appreciated folks, do you know of a fire walk coming up locally that I could take part in and random question – any folks out there who could teach me to ride a unicycle? That's got to be worth seeing!

I did manage a couple of challenges this week, 26 completed now. With the help of Coach Alison and a newbie opponent Allan, we try our hand a racket ball. Never played before and was great fun and I am not sure I can keep the running up as often as I do for much longer and racket ball could be the future, or I could put my feet up, I think not.

Yesterday, it was a pleasure and great privilege to be the eyes and guide Maggie on one of her training run for the Milton Keynes marathon later in the year. Under the watchful eye and fabulous help and support of Ellen, Maggie's regular guide, we headed out for few miles in the beautiful Warwickshire countryside. The conversation flowed as we talked about life and its meaning remembering to give Maggie an instruction or two to keep her safe. Talk about trust, I felt at ease with Maggie and was aware that I had a job to do and was not a game for her or another tick in the box, this was her freedom. I have absolute respect for both Maggie and Ellen and the bond between them was evident, bringing a tear or two to my eye. As we ran, we talked then out the blue, Ellen said "let the guide rope go and let Maggie run free". With a guide either side and safe path ahead, Maggie was away. Her face showed everything, having some to help and guide her was fine, but what she really wanted was to do this by herself.

When I look at the great work that Helping Hands do, most of the folks that Lianne and the team help just want to "run free" but just need that direction or someone just being there.

The journey continues.......

HALF TIME

Passing the halfway point of the challenge year, I subconsciously felt the pressure increasing. I like numbers and data, maybe it's a man thing, keeping a watchful eye on the stats I knew I was behind. I knew I had set myself a difficult task and really wanted to keep to the plan but that is not always so easy. The hidden challenge that I had taken on was juggling not only a full-time job and family commitments, but approximately a run with a new person every week and a challenge off the list as well. Way back in December 2016, when I announced to Julie my idea, she did ask me what I was going to give up so I could take on 56 challenges in a year. I hadn't really cleared to decks so a bulging schedule should not come as a surprise. Maybe that is what was making the journey worth taking, some of the experiences that I have already had were life changing and with five months to go, looking forward made my pulse race and reach for the planner and my laptop, time to up my game.

Saturday 27th January 2018 - Teach a man to fish

I am no expert on the bible but I do like the quote "give a man a fish and you feed him for a day; teach a man to fish and you feed him for life". Thinking about it I am not even sure that it's from the bible. I might be getting my fish quotes mixed up but the idea of people helping people is not new.

When I saw a post on social media from Helping Hands recently, it struck a chord – "Our soup kitchen isn't just about the food, it's a meeting place, a time to build relationship/friendships, and a safe place where people feel they belong and are welcome. It's also a time where we are able to listen and assess what further support they need."

So much more than giving out fish and as the 56notout journey continues, the more I see people helping people.

As I ramp up the pressure for the final few months, I would like to say thank you for sticking with me and appreciate the help and support.

I am still looking to bring some challenges home; fire walking is playing hard to get and any one heard from Daniel Craig?

Run #38 – David Morecroft OBE

I have said before that I am ok with people, but I was a little nervous as I walked into the reception of the Xcel Leisure Centre. I was about to run with David Morecroft OBE, this guy ran 5000 metres in 13:00.41 minutes, the world record set in 1982 at the Bislett Games in Oslo and stood for three years until broken by Saïd Aouita (although it remained a British record until 2010). He remains the last non-African to set a 5,000 m world record. What a gentleman, as we ran we chatted and he was as interested in me as much as I was of him. I did glance across to David a couple of times as we ran in the suburbs of Coventry and secretly pinched myself. I am running with David Morecroft, David Morecroft! I don't get star struck, I am fortunate to have met many famous people over the years and generally they are just normal people that are just well known, but David was famous for being the best at his craft and that was different for me. David was open, talking about the early days and the passion for the sport that had looked after him all his life and spawned the whole new career in media that is now making him a familiar face to another generation of wannabe athletes and sports fans alike. Maybe David could get me on the telly, got to be worth asking.....

I loved the end of run video David and I did together, the warmth from our time together was clear. A true gentleman and an experience that would give me bragging rights for many years to come.

10th February 2018 - Running to stand still

It has been a funny week in camp 56notout with some dates firmed up for future challenges and some that I thought were in the bag are not but progress nevertheless.

We are delighted that the sale of the calendars has raised over £400 which has been split between the two great charities, thank you to everyone who supported the cause. Proud that the "Street life" photographs are on the wall are from as far afield as Sweden, Germany and Michigan, North America. A rewarding challenge that was not on the original list has turned out to be a great example of teamwork.

Hearing the stories of the support that people are giving people gives me the drive to keep going .especially as the marathon looms ever closer and the weekly training miles necessary start to climb, but a great chance to spread the word as running friends, new and old, become a captive audience while keeping me company.

With a change in pace comes a change in attitude and for the first time for many years, I decided to put a tie on for work, and was surprised at the change in people's perception of me. This made me realised that I have a choice and as in previous blogs, not everyone has the same options. Appearances make a difference. As you walk past that guy on the street corner, you rarely see the person behind the dirty cloths and stubbly chin. The local centres where folks can drop in and be themselves make such a difference.

As the awareness spreads, try to look beyond what you see and look for the person inside. You might be surprised what you see.

Take cover!

I have no idea how this challenge ended up on the list, it was there from day one mainly because I thought it was impossible to arrange. By their very nature, a tank is not something that people generally have in the garage. One of the new people that I had to pleasure to meet was Helen, a community champion from Tesco's, who just had a great life skill of just making stuff happen so over a coffee, we chatted and I shared my challenge list with her. Sitting back and listening to my story and the wacky things I had planned, Helen sat quietly and occasionally scribbled on the pad. I could hear the cogs ticking but she just said, leave it with me. On 2nd October 2017 out of the blue, I had a communication from my Tesco friend, "I've got a little something for you, actually it's huge!" read the message, with a photo and everything.

Helen had managed to find some who had a tank and was willing to let me have a go in it. It took a while to sort out the final details and thought waiting for the better weather would be a good idea so with Christmas out of the way it was all systems go. The directions to the location where the tank lived were a little woolly so airing to the side of caution, I arranged to pick Helen up. As we drive into the back of beyond, we saw a sign. Here you go, it down here and as we pulled into a parking space, Mick came out the house to meet us. What a gentleman, within seconds, I felt like I had known him for years. Mick told us that the Walton family have had a longer relationship was transport with the passion shared with his grown-up children and grandchildren - a real family affair.

Walking around the yard, chatting to his lad and looking at all the vehicles that was his life, I spotted a tank, hiding in one of the sheds. It was bloody massive, and this was only a baby. My blog post later in the day gives you all the data. Climbing onto the tank, I somehow realised the scale of the beast. It might sound obvious, but Mick pointed out that nothing on this vehicle was soft. If I slipped, whatever I landed on, was hard and would hurt. No soft refinement of the family saloon, becoming more apparent as I dropped into the driver's seat. As the engine roared into life, the power took me by surprise and as happened with the JCB some weeks before, another Mick gave me on the job instructions.

A completely different kettle of fish this time, two levers sturdy levers in lieu of a steering wheel and these were soon to become my first introduction to the force required just to make this thing move. Mick soon refined my gentle approach to handling the tank into one requiring a little more muscle. The smile on my face was from ear to ear and realised that I could soon do a lot of damage. A thought-provoking lesson was until I (man) brought the machine to life, the heavyweight fighting machine along with its weaponry, was harmless. Helen, up to now, was filming the challenge and clearly having as much fun as me, happily stood by and watched. "Any chance of letting Helen have a go Mick?". The smile transferred from my face to hers as I happily changed roles.

Mick's passion and the clear love of his family became even more apparent as we had the tour of the "club house". An enormous shed and the hub of the Walton family's world, games and a bar plus tanks too.

An incredible morning.

ANOTHER CURVED BALL, ALTHOUGH I HOPED IT WASN'T

It's was mid-February, six weeks into the dreaded marathon training and I had the early signs of a problem. For many, marathon training is a way of life and something to be done but for me I do not enjoy the pressure and the regular increase in the weekly mileage. Anyone would be foolish to stand on the start line without doing the training. The number of training plans probably equal the number of runners who take part. Work, family and life in general are all influences that play their part in the months after Christmas, you know, the first few months of a new year when the days are short, the weather is cold and wet with a pretty good chance of snow and in my case, carrying the excesses of the festive period around my middle.

The plan I had was tried and tested with a steady increase in the miles but still a shock to the system and once the miles hit double figures, my pelvis muscles started to object and at times, I could barely walk post run. Not a good start and I was worried that one of the big challenges of the year was under threat, not forgetting that I had already committed to raising £2000 for Shelter so no going back. After a spontaneous check up at the Birmingham Running Show, after an observant physiotherapist notice me hobbling past with my daughter Libby and whipped me on to his couch, I knew it was time to contact my fellow runner and trained physiotherapist, Bethan.

Hi Bethan, I hope you are well? I need your professional help!!!!! It looks like I might have a problem that could do with looking at, running related of course.

We talked later the same day and soon I was taking her advice and the exercises that she recommended to get me back on plan albeit a new less dramatic training routine. Time would tell if I was going to be ok but I invested in new trainers almost as a symbolic act of commitment.

17th February 2018 – Love not war

OK, not all the challenges are hard and some of them I have done have been a lot of fun but even so, very thought provoking. I was delighted to tick another challenge off today when with the help of Helen Willoughby and Mick and Lee Walton I got to drive a 16 ½ ton tank or a Vickers FV433 self-propelled gun to be precise and it made a lovely change from running. Such a powerful beast, but got me thinking, that in the wrong hands, and with the ability to fire shells that I could barely lift over ten miles was pretty scary, and this was tiddler as far as tanks go. Even the sheer mass of the body powered by a mighty Rolls Royce engine that would run on anything for fuel could do a lot of damage; the word "respect" came to mind.

But you do not need a tank to do damage, the pen is mightier that the sword as the quote goes – so true but by the same token, little acts of kindness can make a massive difference too. I would not want to be on the streets at any time, but the last few days have been bloody freezing, I am so grateful for those who are looking out for those who do not have a choice, like the passers-by who, in the news this week are taking a man living in a phone box in the Midlands, food and warm clothing. Hearing of his situation, although it made me sad, it also made me angry. It is the 21st Century and we are a developed country, am I missing something?.... a man having to live in a phone box ?!!

Runs #39,40,41 – Karen Lines, Claudine Olney, Jaymie Icke

I planned to go for the hat trick today, three runners in one day equals three runs. I am training for a marathon so I should be able to pull this off. A lovely mix of people today, my first runner was someone I had never met before and yet another one of Helen's intros. I had arranged to meet Karen at Leamington Parkrun and although we were amongst many other runners taking part in the weekly run fest it didn't matter. Strange to say but the other runners didn't matter, this was our run and we were in our own little bubble. I liked Karen from the off, she buzzed not like a bee but full of life or Joie de Vivre as the French say. The true translation is keen or buoyant enjoyment of life. We talked out the challenge year completely oblivious to everyone around us but as we entered the last part of the route, I was aware that we were attracting a little attention. I'll run with you and I might be able to help you, I work on the radio. Happy to add another runner to my ever-growing list and delighted to meet a potential useful contact, I wanted to finish the run with Karen and grab a coffee. Completely unphased with waiting her turn, I introduced myself properly to my parkrun stalker. It turned out to be no other than Kirstie Leahy from Touch FM and although we would get to run together but not yet, our paths would keep crossing, but not today, I had another runner to meet and something very out of context for both of us. Usually when we meet, I am singing the low notes and Claudine belts out nothing ever resembling the tune. We both sing in the same choir and during rehearsals, we stand within ear shot of one another. (Claudine is an alto, alto 1 to be precise and altos rarely get to sing the tune) This morning, neither Claudine or I needed to worry about hitting a bum note and we could have a sensible conversation whist enjoying the stunning weather as we completed a few circuits of Victoria Park.

New to running and clearly enjoying the sense of achievement that comes with completing another mile, Claudine certainly has been bitten by the running bug. Apart from the choir, I was surprised on how many mutual friends that we had in common and always makes me marvel at the thread of life and a small world we live in. My third and final run of the morning was very much closer to home in the form of my nephew and active supporter of Shelter, Jaymie Icke. Since moving off his childhood home of the Isle of Wight to Derby, we do get to see each other a lot more and my sister too which is a bonus in some ways but does negate the need to visit this beautiful island off the south coast of England. Jaymie was born in Leamington, the next town to where I live now so it was pretty much like coming home for him.

He loves it around here and has threatened to move back in the past but know he and his fiancée Beth have made Derby home. Jaymie certainly gave me a run for my money and was lovely to have some time together just the two of us but we (actually me) did make a pigs ear of the mid run video and on arriving home realised I had only taken a couple of selfies so out in the garden for take two.

We would meet up again later the same day for a family gathering and the last few beers I would be having for a while.

Congratulations Emma and Bolo on your engagement.

GET ON THE WAGON!

A little maths was involved with this challenge, 56 days without any alcohol and for this idea I had hoped that I would get some help and support from the family but not a chance! I had perused my diary for a while to work out the best time to go without a drink but seemed to be always something that would enviably push me off the wagon. Obvious occasions like Christmas and New Year, but also holidays and family gatherings where the wine would flow, and I would not be so keen in missing out on a glass of something but a great coincidence came along with two events in the diary with exactly 56 days between them. Emma and Bolo's engagement party and the London Marathon - perfect. At around 11.30pm at the party, I ordered my last pint and enjoyed making a somewhat slurry video blog complete with boozy cheers from the party goers as midnight approached. The next alcoholic drink would be the other side of the finishing line in London.

How I got on, will have to wait .....

25th February 2018 - Lord kill the pain

Lord Kill the pain, just until tomorrow. Get up in the morning, breakfast from a bottle – Pig Iron

I have always liked these lyrics and a passing comment did make me think that if I lived on the streets, I would want something to help kill the pain. I have never been a big drinker, in fact I'm pretty rubbish at it to be honest, but at the end of a busy week, I do like to have a glass or two of something to mark the arrival of the weekend. Today is the start of another challenge 56 days to complete, as I go tee total for a couple of months, the next time I have an alcoholic drink will be on the other side of the London Marathon. Just before midnight, I had my final beer for a while and will be interesting to see how this change will impact not only my health, waistline and pocket. We have several family events coming up where a glass of something would help mark the occasion and also some challenges where a drink to calm the nerves would be appreciated. But no one said it would be easy, fancy giving it ago?

The week has been busy in camp 56notout with a chance to meet some great new people, fabulous support from the media and more to come hopefully, following a spontaneous interview at Leamington Park Run, and a lovely message from our local MP, thanks Matt, plus confirmation of dates for future challenges.

Don't look down!

If there was any day so far that the support of some Dutch courage would help, it was this morning but alas, no alcohol for me this morning. The challenge year was always going to take me out of my comfort zone at times and test my fears. I have already tackled water, performing in public along with others but today I was taking on my fear of heights.

The drive over to the Warwick university campus on the outskirts of Coventry, the location of today's challenge was tough enough in itself having snowed overnight and freezing with the dawn, making the roads very difficult to drive on. Arriving at Warwick Sport, it seemed that my contact had been impacted by the overnight freeze as he travelled to work by motorbike, but my visit was logged and Richard Kendrick, another instructor stepped in to help. I had arranged to be met by Selina Welter, Warwick Sport's marketing executive at the time, who was keen to promote the visit and the 56notout challenge and recorded the morning to be made into a video.

The walk into the climbing hall, my nerves did not calm at all. The cavernous room was intimidating and glad that we were the only climbers heading upwards this morning. Having already been kitted out with shoes and harness, it was time to get off the floor. With Richard on the end of the safety rope, I questioned the logic as he was half my weight and if I slipped, I had visions of Richard rocketing to the ceiling as I plummeted in the opposite direction but I was reassured that it did not work like that and pulleys along with the laws of physics would come into play. I could tell that this was not the first time he had been asked that question. Trust, I have spoken of trust many times and today I was putting my trust in Richard and the equipment but also trust in my own ability and nerve.

As I climbed, Richard took the slack in the safety rope and coached me ever upwards, looking down I was high enough for my first climb. Ok, lean back Steve and just sit on the rope, shit that was a strange feeling, back to trust again. Once I had convinced myself that I was actually not going to test the laws of gravity and plummet to the ground, I wall walked (not sure if that is the real name) back to the temporary sanctuary of the ground. Ok, Richard announced, have another go but this time only use the orange blocks and get as far as that ridge, ok no pressure then. Focussing on the orange blocks and the destination, I forgot about the height and my fear. "Very clever Richard", I shouted down - mind games, very good.

I shouldn't have looked down and all the time Selina was filming. I was starting to relax a little and even enjoy myself but aware of the time and the day ahead I wanted to have a go at abseiling.

Whist Richard got ready; Selina wanted to interview me. I was getting the hang of telling the story and doing the sales pitch, I just hoped the camera couldn't pick up my knees knocking! Selina prompted me with questions and just let me do the rest, my passion and continued enthusiasm taking over. Interview done, over to Richard who had prepared the next challenge. My face must have been a picture when he pointed out the anchor point that he had attached some 5 metres up the wall and was to where I was to climb to then abseil down. "Don't I get a practice?" I asked - nope, came the reply. You are doing great, he reassured me, yet more "on the job" training.

Having been talked through what I needed to do on the ground, it was time to do this for real, with Richard on the end of my safety rope, I made my way to the anchor point, I stopped but unfortunately I had to go a few more feet before I was waist level. Then came the tough point, taking the rope from the anchor point and attaching it to the belay device. Richard was calling out the instructions, but I was panicking, my heart rate was through the roof. Deep breaths Steve, you can do this. I attached the rope and sat back in the harness, I was now on the rope that would take me to the ground and the decent was in my hands. My legs were like jelly and glancing down realising how high I was not a good idea. More deep breaths and I started to make my way down, elegant and confident it was not but I made it back to earth in one piece and without having a heart attack.

Shaking Richard's hand and a hug from Selina, my fear was apparent. "You really are shaking" proclaimed Richard! Oh yes, that was a massive leap of faith for me, but I enjoyed it. After saying my thankyou's, I headed back into the cold proud of what I had done. I would love to give it another go, I think. Unaware of anything going on around me, a few days later Selina's video arrived and was amazing and inspired me to learn how to produce these myself but that would have to wait for another time.

SNOW ANGEL

I do love a bit of spontaneity, to grab people's attention you cannot beat a bit of bare flesh and humiliation so waking up to another falling of snow I seize the moment. body coordination is not one of my strong points and thought that a snow angle would give it a test but does make good telly as they say. So on with beach shorts and sunglasses and I was ready.

My youngest was up and about so a quick check that she would be ok with this latest exploit. I am always aware of the impact I have on my family but still need to be reminded that what I am doing is very public and need to ensure that those close to me done not suffer in any way from the fallout of my exploits especially Millie who is still at school albeit in the final year of sixth form, but today she was ok with what I had planned and also provided the birds eye photo of my wacky snow angle in the back garden. Laying in the freezing snow in a pair of shorts took my breath away and my first attempt at a snow angle was not a classic but it did get folks talking on social media and showed everyone that I do not take myself too seriously.

Never far away from the reason why I had embarked on this crazy journey, the reality of harsh weather conditions not always a welcome distraction. Snow can be a lot of fun and looks great on Christmas cards or posters advertising skiing holidays but by its very nature, it's cold and wet and not good to spend your days in.

I would not want to spend my life without a roof over my head regardless of the weather and dry warm clothes to wear along with the same criteria for the place to sleep should be a given in this day and age. Homelessness is not a lifestyle choice for most people and sleeping under the stars sounds romantic but not when it's the only game in town. The tv and radio news was full of the tragic consequences of the combination of freezing temperatures and a life on the streets with many dying in ever increasing numbers.

The increased awareness of the plight of those less fortunate did come with positive actions from local authorities opening offices and shelters plus the increased activities of charities fuelled by the actions and donations of the general public and business alike. My heart warmed by the generosity and kindness from the good folks of this world offsetting the drop-in temperatures on the streets of our towns and cities.

Wanting to wrap up warm myself, I soon realised that I had more than enough hats, gloves and scarves to last me a lifetime, time for a little de cluttering and put the various winter accessories gathering dust in wardrobe to better use. The coat rack idea of Helping Hands, a simple rail strategically located outside stores and in the receptions of companies offering passing members of the public and employees a place to put warm clothing for the benefit of others.

3rd March 2018 – Trust

Boy its cold outside and if you're out on the streets, a sky full of the white stuff is the last thing you need. it does give me a warm feeling that we are all realising that we can all do something to help, either directly or by helping the many charities who know what to do and know where the need is, and I continue to be moved seeing the good in people.

It's been another busy week in the 56notout camp with another three challenges off the list, making a total of 30 done and another 3 underway. A week down without a drink with another 7 weeks to go and I would have appreciated a drink this week, that's for sure.

One of my biggest fears is heights, and with the help of Richard and the great people at Warwick Sports on the University of Warwick campus, I put on my climbing shoes and headed upwards. It was all about trust for me and at the tender age of 56 I do like to be in control, and with Richard at the end of the safety rope and him having all the answers, I could do little else but put my trust in him. An amazing life lesson and a wonderful experience learning yet more about myself and just what I am capable of, and more importantly, spreading the word and awareness.

I could tell that as we discussed the challenge and those I had already done, along with the great things arranged in the diary for the last few months of the challenge, I could sense the genuine interest, and as usual the passion became apparent as I had to wipe a little moisture from the corner of my eyes. Or maybe it was just sheer terror!

So dig out those spare pairs of gloves, excess drawers of hats, wardrobes of coats and head down to your local charity and give someone some warmth. Hope springs eternal..

With most of the snow melted away, at least around my home, there are signs that spring might just be around the corner, along with the hope of warmer weather. I love the spring and always feel it is a time for hope and a fresh beginning.

Warmth for me is not just about the physical temperature, it is also the warmth showed by people to each other, with the shops awash with flowers and gifts for our mothers, it reminded me of an old Chinese proverb. A little fragrance always clings to the hand that gives the roses. On the 56notout journey, my contact with people is the best part of the challenge. The help and support that continues to be offered is just the best thing, as I enter what I feel will be a manic phase of the challenge, as I progress many of the ideas to a result. I have yet to come across anyone who is against helping others, although some ideas of the form this takes can vary, and sometimes results in some heated discussions.

Some challenges are still a little elusive, and I would still like to give fire walking a go, ideally after the London marathon which is only six weeks away, and I have realised I have no challenges involving animals, any ideas – shear a sheep maybe? And come on Daniel Craig, you know you want to run with me! May is going to be a little crazy I think but I know it will be worth it, and at least the bar will be open again following my (hopefully) 56 alcohol free days, and the team are in the planning stage of a party in the summer, watch this space!

The brilliant video so kindly produced by Selena from Warwick Sport has helped promote the challenge so please give it a watch.

RUN #42 – FATEMA EL-ZAHRAA EL-WAKEEL

To be able to spend time with someone from another country always adds a new dimension to life and to see the world from a different perspective. Fatema is from Egypt, born in Alexandra but has made England her home. For today's run, I decided to put on my tour guide hat and share the stunning backwaters and stories from my hometown. The obvious view of Warwick Castle from the bridge over the Avon is difficult to avoid and why would you want to avoid this spectacular photo opportunity. I would not even like to hazard a guess on how many people have taken the very same photo from the very same spot over the years. I know I can never resist the chance to take a photo whenever I cross the bridge, always a different sky or mood. A view I will never tire of and surprisingly one that Fatema had never noticed before even though she has driven over the bridge many times.

As well as the obvious tourist attractions, I wanted her to see the hidden gems of this amazing town, the route I planned was based on my go to standard Saturday run and could do in my sleep and often do. I like the contrast and the calm of Bridge End, the view of course and then down Mill Street to one of my favourite places in Warwick, the beautiful Mill Gardens. The horticultural sanctuary in the shadow of the 44.8-metre-tall Caesar's Tower. The gardens are open to the public and a place I love visit at any time of the year. I suspect Fatema will return and see for herself but today we run and returning up the cobbled street and immediately into the gateway to the castle, skirting the ticket office and through the tiny gate in the wall and into town, into the square with its weekly Saturday market in full swing then into Barrack Street giving me a chance to recount the chilling story of its past. The short street used to be known as Bridewell Lane because the House of Correction or Bridewell stood on one side of it. On the opposite side stood the County Gaol which was later to become a barracks, hence the street name change. The bricked-up archway used to be the site of public executions. The small dark marks each side of the arch and above it show where the scaffold was fixed to the wall along with two small rings in the wall either side of the arch and one in the chapel opposite where chains were fixed to keep the crowds under control when executions were carried out, the only indications of the streets gruesome past. Warwick gaol moved to a new site in Cape Road in 1861 and the last public execution in England was in 1868. Not sure when the last hanging took place in Warwick.

With the stories coming thick and fast as we ran, we headed along tink-a-tank, the perimeter path around saint Mary's church yard. Fatema slowed to a walking pace, "We should not run with these graves, Steve. We will disturb those who are asleep." I like this sentiment and since then, I walk through churchyards.

With the town centre behind us, we headed across priory park shortcutting to St Johns House, a Jacobean mansion which has a history spanning almost 900 years. The land on which it stands was originally used as a hospital in the 12th century. The current house has been used as a private residence, a school and administrative offices of the War Department and now a fabulous learning resource used by local schools with its galleries, Victorian kitchen and schoolroom along with a great display of childhood, toys and games, costumes. On the first floor of the house is The Royal Warwickshire Regiment of Fusiliers Museum. My favourite part is the gardens, very peaceful considering that hustle and bustle of Warwick is only a walls thickness away.

The gardens became the backdrop for the obligatory video. With the media stuff done, we headed for home via Saint Nicholas Park. How many saints in one run!

Run #43 – Oliver Bates

I was preaching to the converted with Oliver, he had already volunteered at the Helping Hands soup kitchen as part of his Duke of Edinburgh silver award wanting to understand how a soup kitchen worked so had experienced the effects of being homeless first hand. Oliver was the second member of the Bates family that I had ran with, in the final years of school, Oliver had his life ahead of him and was in the midst of planning his future. A lot more difficult than I was at his age with considerably more choices on offer. I reckon that Oliver had a plan but was keeping his options open. Already had the benefit of travel to broaden his outlook on life having been born in Barcelona, Spain before returning to the UK with his family via Shanghai, China. I think Oliver knows there is a big wide world out there and I liked his compassion that he clearly had for others.

RUN #44 – PADDY KIRKMAN

It was the modern feminist anthem "Sisters Are Doin' It for Themselves" written by Eurythmics members Annie Lennox and David A. Stewart and recorded in 1985 as a duet by the British pop duo Eurythmics and American singer Aretha Franklin, that immortalised the words "behind every great man there has to be a great woman" but can work the other way around. Paddy is Helping Hands CEO Lianne Kirkman's, other half and whist Lianne is at the helm of the good ship Helping Hands, Paddy is in the engine room. They make a good team and although always in the thick of the action, tends to step to the side when the camera appears unless there is a guitar to be played or a song to be sung, then it's a completely different kettle of fish. Paddy loves his music and we have many friends in common, working in the same industry bring another selection of common acquaintances. Highlighted when we exchange trainers for two wheels for a couple of cycling based challenges, more about the second one later. I could tell that Paddy was not a big fan of running, so with that in mind, we kept our run short and sweet.

18th March 2018 – London Calling!

A bit chilly out there, but with 5 weeks until London, I need to get out for a run. I am lucky; I have the choice whether or not to go out in it.

I am taking advantage of an afternoon in my PJ's today, (sorry for that mental image!) it's a great time to do some planning and getting some future challenges in the diary. With some great responses to my appeal for help on Facebook which I will be following up on during the next few days, I thought I might let you know what is in the diary so far, as support during the challenges is a great help.

Friday 23rd June sees two challenges in 24 hours, kicking off with a Bush Tucker Challenge at LAC, when I take on the apprentices at work , followed by a Sunset to Sunrise walk, 20 miles through the night, and also ticks off a challenge for the guy whose idea I borrowed, but more about him next time.

On Good Friday, with the help of Helen from Tesco I will be attempting 56 miles on an exercise bike in store dressed as the Easter Bunny, followed by my stage debut the following night playing the trombone with Chain of Fools at the Riverside in Stratford, bring ear plugs to wear during my bit if you're coming along, and then it will be into the final few weeks before the marathon, and the appearance of Saint George !

I hope to take on the big seven rollercoasters at Alton Towers in April, take to the pitch at the Ricoh Stadium with Wasps on the 14th and I am delighted to be running in the ketchup outfit in my home town of Leamington Spa in the annual Regency Run on Sunday 15th April.

Looking further ahead , hoping to have a week off from running after The London Marathon during which I will drink large amounts of alcohol having (hopefully) completed the challenge of 56 alcohol free days before I will be back in the Ketchup outfit with my eldest daughter Libby in the mustard outfit for the Leeds Half marathon on 13th May.

I am planning to cycle from London to Leamington and need some folks to join me with a provisional date of Saturday 19th May, please let me know if you want to join me for some or all of the steady 100 ride and the next day, a colour blast run with my daughter Millie.

Saturday 30th June, with the year of challenges over it will be time to party!! More details to follow but please save the date.

Stay warm everyone.

RUN #45 – KENILWORTH RUNNERS

I felt like I was taking a trip to the dark side when I arrived at the Wardens cricket club, HQ of Kenilworth Runners, friendly rivals of my old club Leamington based Spa Striders from the next town some 5 miles away. Meeting Stewart Underhill, who had offered to run with me via Facebook, I soon realised that he was the chairman and I might just have a bit of company on our run. Once Stewart completed the welcome spiel, traditional with club nights, I was given a brief introduction and a chance to thank the assembled mass for having me, a group photo before joining a group more suitable for my ability, I never saw the rest of them again. I liked running with a bigger group again, I could mingle and with a captive audience, could spread the 56notout message. I had got this down to a tee now and could recite my sales pitch without thinking too hard. The group I was with were receptive to my story and the miles passed without too much trouble, happy that I had joined the right group. I never did get to run with Spa Striders although I did run with plenty of the club members, maybe next time.

Run #46 – Gary Mathews

Now did Gary have a story or what! Gary was a relatively new member of the Helping Hands team, running the Gateway Cafe in Warwick. An initiative to provide a platform for personal development and also provide some great food for the good people of Warwick. The Gateway Café helps people to regain their confidence and gain new skills giving people support and opportunities to gain qualifications and get work. Although Gary enjoyed working in the Cafe, I could clearly see that his passion lies elsewhere. Discovering Christianity whilst in prison, the calling to use his newly found faith and building on the experiences of his own chequered life, Gary would be a natural minister working at the coal face. I could not see him as the vicar at a village church in middle England but in the thick of blood and guts in a deprived inner city where hope and charity along with someone who had hit the bottom and is on the way up means so much more than pompous do gooders. As Gary talked openly about his life, his struggles with drug addiction and numerous visits to prison, he was clearly a fighter in more ways than one. With the odds so heavily stacked against him, my money would have been on a sad and lonely outcome ending in dirty squat or under the arches of a damp railway track but Gary's life was to heading in a completely different direction and I would have lost my shirt, not that I am a gambling man anyway. I listened intently as Gary gave me the abridged version of his life story, so very different from my own but very glad that our paths had been brought together, with the challenge year in its final couple of months, to run with someone who had "been there, done that" so to speak was a welcome boost. We agreed to run again and I am sure Gary promised me a bacon butty after, I need to take him up on that offer maybe when his journey has progressed a little further.

When looking at the cafe details on the internet, I reckon Gary might have written the words ......

"The Helping Hands Gateway Cafe is a life changing experience - not only does it help with qualifications and experience it helps with confidence and mental health. It's also an amazing place to be with amazing staff who support you and the cafe is a religious and spiritual place where you can relax and with the help of friends and God can be able to express yourself without judgement. Helping Hands changes so many lives it's an amazing charity and I am honoured to be part of the Helping Hands family."

THE DARKER THE NIGHT, THE BRIGHTER THE LIGHT

I had mixed feelings about this challenge, when the idea was first tabled, I mis-heard the intention. I thought Nigel said to walk from sunrise to sunset which sounded ok, a good days walk, I was up for that but soon realised that the challenge was not as I thought, the opposite in fact, sunset to sunrise-through the night, now that was a different kettle of fish. We had planned to do this at the end of last year in the days between Christmas and New Year but we had to change the date due to illness in both families so with the absence of a natural holiday, we plumped for Friday night in March.

Nigel had sorted out the route and the logistics of transport overcome once I had cajoled a good friend to forsake his bed at some ungodly hour and pick us up. For the first few miles we had both an extra member of the team and the half-light even though the sun had gone down but by the time we reached the outskirts of Meriden we said farewell to both the final dregs of daylight and Alfie the border terrier who had been picked up to spend the night snuggled up in his basket. From now until dawn, the moon and artificial light would illuminate our path. To break the long night, we planned stops to refuel. The Queens Head at Meriden, the official start and finish of the annual Coventry Way challenge but tonight providing the first chance of a comfort stop, I could have murdered a beer but as I was still in the thick of my dry period so I had to I settled on watching Nigel drink his pint whilst I nursed a soft drink.

Staying in the village of Meriden, until recent times, the village was believed to be the geographical centre of England

and furthest point from the British coastline, but this was disproven by Ordnance Survey in the early-2000s but still claims the honour. We sat on a bench and devoured our fish and chips before heading off road and into the Warwickshire countryside under the light of our head torches.

From the churchyard of Saint Lawrence's church, Coventry made a spectacular sight bathing the sky in orange whist adding to the contrast of the darkness at the edge of town. The route we had chosen was to walk just over half of the Coventry Way, a forty-mile circular around the City and the green and white route markers leaped out to be spotted by the bright beams from our LED headlights and continued to guide our way. Once we arrived in Burton Green, we knew we had an easy few miles ahead of us as we dropped onto the disused railway line, better known as the Greenway, that would take us to the edge of Kenilworth. Turning a horse mount into a picnic table, we stopped for a coffee and a bit of cake as Friday crossed into Saturday. I love a bit of cheese, the literal kind, and against Julie's plea, I used a phrase I had been desperate to use for a while and became the title of my blog the following morning.

Refilled and passing a few houses still showing signs of life we continued our journey now other side of midnight. Skirting the centre of Kenilworth the route took Nigel and I across the fairways of Kenilworth golf club which must really piss off the golfers on a summers afternoon as marauds of ramblers heavy booted take to the greens but tonight we had the course to ourselves with no chance of being hit by a stray ball. In the early hours of the morning the threat of rain became real but was only a light shower and not enough to dampen our spirits. The conversation continued and we covered a wide spectrum of subjects as I alluded to in my blog the following morning.

I have always enjoyed Nigel's company since we met back in mid-eighties sharing many adventures during the last thirty plus years and still do so. Fitting to share this experience together as without the intricate thread of life and the path it takes, the 56notout challenge would not have been. Arriving in the village of Ryton on Dunsmore, we were both glad to see my buddy Ian to take us home to our warm beds....

24th March 2018 - The other side of midnight

Last night I ticked another challenge off the list and one with real significance. I have mentioned before that the original idea for the year of challenges came from a friend of a my lifelong friend Nigel who had planned on doing a year of challenges to celebrate his birthday and raise money for a charity close to him, but unfortunately Stuart became ill and could not complete his list so his friends came to the rescue, picked up the gauntlet and carried on, sharing the list between them. Nigel seized the chance to help a friend and was only fitting that I did the selected challenge with him and added the same idea to my list. When I first heard the plan, I was keen, walk from Sunrise to Sunset, doddle I thought, but I misheard the words. Sunset to Sunrise, a twelve hour walk through the night, now that was a different kettle of fish, it would be dark and two grown men walking across country in the middle of the night with head torches wouldn't attract attention at all would it?

We planned to do a section of the Coventry Way to give the walk a defined start and finish and as the sun set, albeit masked by cloud, headed off with the green sign and a big printed map to guide our way. For the first few miles we had Alfie, Nigel's dog along for the walk and the conversation flowed and although it did slow up at times, especially in the early hours of a rainy Saturday morning, the subjects of discussion were varied, including the rise and fall of Ant and Dec, which was random for two men in the later years of their fifties. We talked of life, past present and future, our parents and our offspring. After a chippy tea and a chase to raise a glass to Stuart (a soft one for me, as still in the dry period!) we headed off into the dark, lights on now and the countryside took on a different perspective. Hitting the Greenway on the outskirts of Burton Green around 11.30pm made for easy walking and side by side we looked forward to a coffee break and a sit down just after mid night. A surreal experience especially as I have ran many times along the Greenway, but never in the dark. The quiet was a nice relief from the hustle and bustle of life but the threat of rain became more apparent, and as the miles passed, we were sure the stiles were starting to get higher, or was that just our legs getting tired?

Ahead of time, the end of the route and running out of maps, the pub came into sight. The dawn chorus began and the first light of a new day made its first appearance. I was hoping for a stunning sunrise but settled for a change to light grey and the promise of a warm bed.

An amazing experience …

Something for the rabbit?

From the outset, I knew that any of the ideas that involved other people would also be a challenge in itself, but as soon as you involve large companies into the mix, the task increases tenfold. I learnt that if I needed help, just ask and then it was all about asking the right person. All pretty obvious stuff I guess but every day's a school day.

Helen from Tesco's was always the right person to talk to and at our first chat over a coffee we talked over doing something in store at Tesco's and after a little brainstorming, the idea of riding an exercise bike dressed as the Easter bunny was born. Helen sorted the admin and I did the rest. Good Friday seemed a good day to take to the saddle, plenty of footfall through the shops man entrance and people in holiday mode with the long weekend in store.

I wanted to have somewhere to go on my static bike ride and Julie suggested Oxford as the virtual destination, a decent enough distance and something people would relate too. Setting up in the foyer of the Southam store, I set off for the university city and the banter started. There is nowt as funny as folk, some people just walked past oblivious to a middle aged man, dressed as a rabbit on an exercise bike but others responded to my comments and if nothing else gave me a smile. People are my life and I was loving chatting to anyone who took the time to chat.

When I meet new people, I try to engage them in the challenge, either a like on Facebook or a potential new challenge or a runner maybe, but just happy with someone to talk to and pass away the miles. Helen and I worked the crowd and "something for the rabbit" became the phrase of the day and the title of my blog the following day.

Especially with the influence of social media, the world is getting ever smaller and always surprises me when the friendship tree throws some interesting and sometimes unexpected connections, today was not exception when a familiar face from my childhood appeared around the corner. I have known Kevin Weller since my days at Cashmore Infants and Junior school, pretty much all my life and as I cycled to Oxford, Kev and I chatted about the old days and the future too. A lovely bonus to the day and gave me food for thought, I would never do half the things I do now in my early years, much preventing staying in the shadows away from the spotlight and has come up a few times over the last few years. I was having far too much fun and before long, I had reached my virtual destination and continued for a few more miles.

The support from friends, old and new along with management of Tesco's was lovely and with a sore backside, it was time to take off the rabbit suit and head home. A great challenge, a chance to spread awareness of the issue of homelessness and put a few quid in the kitty, every little helps!

31st March 2018 - Something for the rabbit?

From a shy child who would not say boo to a goose, I have grown into a bit of a showman in my old age and love people. So having been set the challenge to be the Easter Bunny in a local supermarket, I knew it would be good fun. A bunny on a bike and the target of "cycling" to Oxford just added to the theatre. Working alongside another great charity fund raiser, the banter was great and double the fun. The chance to chat to passing shoppers, explaining the challenge and the great work my two charities do and the need of the homeless in our area made the miles fly by, and before long I had passed Oxford and kept on going. My donation bucket was attracting the spare change from the customers and "have you something for the rabbit" from Helen if a little prompt was needed.

The generosity and warmth from the shoppers and staff of Tesco Southam was a great boost in the last few months of the challenge year, more money in the kitty, and another challenge off the list.

Meeting up with an old school friend who I had known since I was five, reinforced my thoughts of how different I was as a schoolboy as we reminisced about out childhood, old classmates and teachers, along with the plan of a reunion. Those 50 odd miles on an exercise bike in Tesco's dressed as the Easter Bunny was a far bigger journey than I had realised.

Seeing the looks on people faces as they walked into the store to be greeted by a middle-aged man dressed as a bunny was great and a smile generally followed.

Thankyou everyone for your support and have a great Easter

RUN #47 – JESS SWEET

Talk about playing hard to get! Getting to run with Jess became a bit of a challenge in itself, the offer to run with me came very early in the challenge year but has taken a while to happen but glad we persevered. Not for the first time, the Coventry War Memorial Park featured in the run and would not be the last. Jess was the sister a friend of our 56notout social media champion, Emma and to be honest don't recall ever knowingly met before but feel sure we would have done or maybe her sister Becky but didn't matter. I think one of the reasons that we hadn't ran until now is that Jess was unsure what to expect, would I be all competitive and sporty? Jess soon realised that our run together would be the polar opposite. We chatted, we laughed, and we ran too but mainly we chatted and laughed covering as seems to be the norm, a myriad of subjects. Jess was somewhat younger than me and I always love to hear about people's hopes and dreams. The world is your oyster these days with opportunities a plenty if you know what you want and where to look, that does tend to be the hard bit. As I have mentioned before, you got to have a plan. Running with Jess was a pleasure and parting, I felt good about the world and I hope Jess did too.

Run #48 – Rachel Baker

My run with Rachel was one of the most memorable of the challenge year for many reasons. The offer to run came out of the blue via Helping Hands Facebook page who regularly shared our 56notout posts updating the many supporters of the charity and appealing for the occasional requests for help. After seeing Rachael's reply to one such appeal, I made contact and arranged to meet. I couldn't see the connection to anyone I knew so was intrigued by the offer to run. Rachel was on social media but no photographs of her so once we had arranged to meet, I was definitely at a disadvantage and would have to rely on her recognising me. I arrived at the entrance to Campion Hills, our agreed meeting point, a little early, eager to meet a new running partner. As several people ran towards me, then without making eye contact or any form of acknowledgement, continued to run past and off into the distance clearly not the person I was waiting for. Patience is a virtue I understand, wasted on me as I am a very much a new type of person allegedly, not sure where people get that idea from but soon the wait was over and at the agreed time, the beaming face of Rachel approached who clearly knew who I was. After the informal introduction we headed off for our run starting with the question I was desperate to ask, what was her motivation to want to run with me? The reply knocked me for six if I am honest and not what I was expecting.... it was a bit of a two-pronged answer. "Well", she said, "I am new to running and find it a great way to lose weight and get fit", and, pausing a moment, "I lost my brother to the streets and I hope wherever he is, there is someone like you helping a charity like Helping Hands looking out for him". I was taken aback and brought to tears;

I was not expecting that response. Her words got under my skin and into my soul, hearing about Rachel's brother made the reason for the challenge year real and very personal. I loved hearing about her plans and the support that Rachel had from her young family and the inspiration she gave them to help others and I felt that the run had got to both of us. These thoughts were confirmed when as she finished writing in my journal and handed it back to I me, I said I hope we get to run together again, and she smiled.

When I got home, I looked at what she had written -

"Steve, wow, you are absolutely amazing for what you've done and are doing! I'm so glad I came across 56notout and I've really enjoyed meeting and running with you this evening, even the big hill. I wish you all the best and hope we meet again, you rock."

I checked with Rachel ahead of pressing the "publish" button and was moved by her reply and have decided to use exactly as written :-

This is so lovely and of course you can use it. I would love for you to add that you inspired me to become a run leader, which I now am. That was totally down to you. Our meeting has changed us both!!

Run #49 – Tony Stinton

I felt on a roll and another new person to run with thanks to Helen from Tesco's. I have like lost count of the number of people that that amazing lady has put me in contact with. Tony was good company, meeting at his home was a coincidence. When Julie and I started the search for somewhere to lay some roots down, we looked at a property in the next street, before finally settling on a house in Warwick.

Not for the first time, my running companion was in the driving seat as we were out in his patch and Tony had a route in mind although the area familiar to me from my childhood with my first school in the same area. Fortunate that we both live in an area where countryside and open spaces never too far away and a chance to run canal side too which I like to do adding a bonus to the route. Tony was clearly a focused athlete and I was grateful for his patience, adjusting his pace to allow me to keep up with him as well as hold a conversation. We talked triathlons and training plans, helping others and the value of good friends.

7th April 2018 - The calm before the storm

If you need something, just ask, so I did and the results have been amazing.

The power of social media can be used for good stuff as well as knowing that folks have put the dustbin out. Some challenges have been a little elusive but thanks to some great people, they are now in the diary and I will certainly be busy in the last 9 weeks of the challenge year.

I still have a few to confirm and new ideas are coming along all the time. With only a couple of weeks until I head to London, the long runs are coming to an end and very soon I will have my life back. Those training miles have been made a lot easier with the support of great friends and the chance to run with new people too, as part of the "run with 56 people" challenge and this is the one that continues to give me most pleasure, hearing about the lives of others and sharing our stories. The diversity of people, along the variety of conversation, you could not make up. We have laughed and there has been a tear or two as well and my faith in humanity has well and truly been restored, giving me the boost, I needed. I appreciate the open and honesty of those who have taken time to run with me, and the request for another run in the future with some touching words in my journal has made the whole 56notout challenge worth all the effort, so thank you.

The next two weeks are going to fly as many longer challenges come to an end (and yes, I can have a drink!) and some big ones come off the list. Please stay with me for the last few weeks and keep the support and great words of support coming. as it does mean a lot to the me and the team ..

TIME TO FACE MY NEMESIS

Apparently, *"Life is a roller coaster just got to ride it"*, according the words of Ronan Keating.

It's true, life does has its up and downs but today's challenge added a few twists and turns too and would have never been on the challenge list if I had my way. Having spent the last 56 years pretty much keeping fun fairs and theme parks at a suitable distance and happy to hold bags and coats and just watch has suited me just fine. I have visited many a well-known venue worldwide with Micky and I on first name terms in Paris, Florida and California but limiting my thrill seeking to the cable cars and trains although I do like a log flume but any ride that twists and turns and I head in the opposite direction. Emma loved the idea of this challenge, a great chance to raise the exposure on social media and once Alton Towers promised to help, she was all over Facebook like a rash.

Once the date was agreed and time off work sorted, there was no going back. This would be yet another challenge that would not be supported by an alcoholic beverage or two although that might not be such a bad thing. The trip to Staffordshire would be a real family affair with even the youngest member of the family Noah, aged 5, donning a 56notout t shirt and trying a rollercoaster or two. No pressure then!

Getting the t shirts should have been a challenge in itself but the team rallied around and come the day, we all would be flying the flag. The morning started with photographs of various family members posing in the logo blazoned t shirts on social media and the day became very real.

The morning was cold and overcast with a real threat of rain so staying in bed would not be a problem. Little chance of that happening clearly and so let's get the day over with.

We had only travelled 16 miles before someone decided to redesign the back of my car resulting in an unscheduled return home to collect the backup car along with a call to the insurance company. That surely was a good enough reason to call the day off but no chance. Collecting the entry passes, fast track passes and the all-important DigiPasses for the evidence photographs kindly sorted by James Gilmore, a PR executive at Alton Towers World and we were all set. I could relax into the day, the bump in the car didn't help but to be honest, I was dreading the day. All my fears and phobias in one day, heights, speed, disorientation but most of all lack of control.

The warmup rides which the whole family went on were ok I guess but somehow, I was sat in my seat on Nemesis, with Julie and Bolo either side of me, my heart was racing. I wanted off but the safety restraint closed over my head and I had lost the control.

What happened in the next few terrifying minutes was out of my hands, I had been assured that the ride would be over in a flash but to be honest, the ride seemed to last a lifetime and the end could not come soon enough. I managed to keep the contents of my tummy down, but my face was green as I climbed out of my seat, sweaty palms and completely disoriented, that was me done for the day. I even dreaded the drive home and the photo captured the fear and dislike of my ride on nemesis, no mistaking that this was way outside of my comfort zone and was my least favourite challenge so far and suspect would stay that way as the year ended.

Once off the ride, I needed to find myself some quite space to gather my thoughts, but I knew that my relationship with rollercoasters had come to an end. Short and memorable as the ride was the opportunity to increase my desire to become an adrenalin junkie went un-claimed and as the colour started to return to my cheeks and my pulse returned to normal, I returned to my role as bag holder and watcher as the family continued to crave the adrenaline rushes.

A good day but one I do not want to repeat in a hurry and just for the record, the car was written off and we never saw it again.

Run #50 – Annie Cox

A run with a different perspective this afternoon. I have run with Annie many times before but never alone. I have known Annie pretty much all her life, school life at least going to the same school as my two albeit slightly different years. I first became friends with Annie's mum and dad through the school's PTA growing into friends away from school and today, the Cox's are a big part of our life.

Annie's mum, Sue was with me at the birth of the challenge and her Dad, Richard has already been my side kick when I did my first and probably my last triathlon but today was all about Annie and I. Annie is a true sportsman, built like an athlete, trains like an athlete, the mindset of an athlete and she competes, she goes all out to win but today she was happy to run with an old man three times her age but it didn't matter. I always like to try and get in the soul of the person I run with and hear about their hopes, dreams and plans for the future.

In addition to being a good athlete, Annie's other passion is music and has started to make her way in the big wide world taking to uni life like a duck to water and clearly loving the freedom that comes with living away from home. Listening to her talk about her new life made me look back on my own youth, I could hear myself say the exact same things over forty years ago when I headed off to the other side of the pond, living away from home for the first time.

We ran a route that I do with Annie's mum Sue regularly and was a surreal experience, we even popped into to see the latest Leamington Studio Artists exhibition at their home in the East Lodge on the banks of the River Leam in Jephson Gardens.

Run #51 – Tess Lukehurst and #52 – Luke Bates

Today, I had the pleasure of running with two people who had agreed to be one of my 56notout runners and although very different people, on both runs it was all about life's journey. Starting the day with Tess, now her journey is a book in itself and maybe a story she should tell herself. I felt that we could be open to each other, we have known each other for years, initially meeting through "Hashing", I was known as Wrong Hole, Tess was Fresh Turd – together we enjoyed following small mounds of flour on a mystery route laid earlier by the hares. Am I making any sense? Google "Hash House Harriers - a drinking club with a running problem" and all will be revealed.

For the next 43 minutes / 6 km we talked, I could tell from the way Tess talked that she was happy with her life now, the struggles of early life making her a stronger person today. We talked about the challenges that lay ahead and those in my own busy year, little did I know that Tess would help me take to the water later in the year. We ran through our hometown, both loving the area we live which always makes putting on the trainers a pleasure. We both had a busy day ahead of us and after a short stop to allow Tess to scribble in my journal before heading off into the thick of the Parkrun team whilst I jumped in my car to meet Luke, the third and final member of the Bates family.

I wasn't sure how this run was going to go if I was honest. Luke is in his first year of university, still a teenager and sometimes interaction between old farts like me and the youth of today can sometimes be difficult but I pride myself on being a good listener and generally can find common ground to get the conversation going. I loved hearing about what the future could hold for Luke and hopefully gaining some trust and that I wasn't really under instruction from his mum and dad, we talked of music. I could see that this is where his passions really lies and not in spreadsheets and financial figures. We talked about hopes and dreams along with the need to keep your options open. I might have said you only live once at some point and you are a long time dead too, I'm sure. You can have a career and enjoy your passions; life is for living but music maybe doesn't pay the bills unless you are Ed Sheeran, so I did try to encourage Luke to do his studies. We talked about running as well and reading his entry in my journal, post run, I must have touched a couple nerves ....

"... you have inspired me to pursue my music as well as run a marathon before I'm 30.

Enjoy and keep being chatty."

Luke was to be the third and final member of the Bates family I had the opportunity to run with, I will save Mark for 60notout!

GAME ON!

All through the challenge year, progress has always been about contacting the right person. Having spent the previous months trying to make contact with the Wasps PR team at the Ricoh, I was on the verge of giving up. The challenge was pretty vague, "appear at a sporting event" and with a very impressive stadium on the doorstep and an approachable responsive premier league rugby club keen to support the community, I thought this would be a good place to start. Once the prestigious new home to Coventry City Football Club and still is but after a catalogue of mismanagement, now better known as the home of Wasps Rugby Club and an amazing job they have done for bringing a great sport to the masses. Never a fan of the game at school or sport generally, the family and I love a trip to the Ricoh. After an "off the cuff" comment at one of my regular catchups with Kirstie at the Leamington courier office, "the sports guy" put me in touch with Paul Smith, Communication - Sport at the Ricoh and result! Game on.

Paul agreed that I could do a lap of the pitch at the end of the game, I could see that he had really gone out of his way to help me against the backdrop of health and safety restrictions and bureaucracy. I had my ketchup outfit and my family with me as we waited to meet Paul pre-match to run through the plan. Match days are understandably busy for Paul so I appreciated him taking a few minutes to touch base and introduce Jacob who would be looking after us. He came to our seats and made the stewards aware of what was happening and with that done, we sat back and enjoyed the game. Wasps were playing Worcester Warriors today and we would sit in our usual seats and even before the game started the friendly banter started between the rival fans.

I like going to the rugby, such a different atmosphere to football and you can get a beer too. Wasps have a mascot, a giant wasp of course called Sting, who during the game circumnavigated the pitch, hi-fiveing with the kids and waving to the crowd. With an impromptu window of opportunity and a chance for a great photo, I got the ketchup outfit on in a flash and down the steps to the edge of the pitch. A great photo for the album and an always welcome bit of PR.

At the end of the game, the promised lap of the pitch and the second window of opportunity and a real bonus, a photo with Joe Launchbury, Wasps Captain and one of the England squads most capped second row was not to be missed. 6' 6" and weighing in a just under 20 stone the guy was a man mountain but a real gentleman and was happy to pose for a photo.

A great afternoon, a win for Wasps and another challenge off the list.

The Lord sent me and the Lord blows my horn

A busy day already, two runs, a trip to the Ricoh and as night falls, it's time to make my stage debut in a soul band. Up to about a few weeks ago, I have never got a note out of anything brass. This was a big challenge for me and like the best ones, this was given to me and was obviously not on the original list.

The challenge came from Hamish Foxley, fellow runner, webmaster for our running group Zero to Hero, versatile musician and all-round good guy, had his work cut out but as it was his challenge, so don't feel too sorry for him folks. Having met up with him on a wet Sunday afternoon to run me through the basics, he let me take the brass beast home so I could practice, I had the mouthpiece in my car and at any opportunity I gave it a blow, but to be honest I couldn't get a note let alone a tune.

The breakthrough came the week before when a change of mouthpiece came faint glimmer of a note and before long the makings of a tune. The gig was the next night, but bad weather and a flooded venue, resulted in an extra week to practice and a change of venue. I would now be feeling good in the upstairs function room with Chain of Fools at the Biggin Hall pub.

Arriving at the Coventry pub, the stage was set but no punters as yet had arrived, so I had chance to meet the band and have run through the night. I would make my guest appearance at the very start of the second half so I had chance to get settled in to the night and chat with friends who had come to support me and the band. I liked the plan, no big introduction, I would just join the band for the opening number of the second half. Looking the part if nothing else, me and the band went on stage and we were off. "I feel good" bellowed front man Tim and before I knew it I was taking a bow and leaving the stage. Short and sweet but what a great feeling, an experience that I was cherish for the rest of my days, a chance to play with one of the hardest working band, if you believe the posters, maybe but a lovely bunch of people.

Today had been another long but memorable day, great chances to spread the word but boy would I sleep tonight.

Hometown boy

The chance to take part in the annual Regency Run, back to where it all began in more ways than one was an opportunity not to be missed. The Leamington 10k organised by the Leamington and district Round Table, this was the first real competitive race I took part in back in 2005 with exception of a couple of fun runs. With a chance of a bit of nostalgia and a chance to run in the town I was born this was to good an opportunity not to miss. Not a challenge as such but I knew the sight of a six-foot bottle of tomato ketchup accompanied by a bright yellow bottle of mustard would turn a head or two. Having been my unofficial wing man at the ketchup outfits first outing at the Two Castles the previous year, Anne was the obvious choice to get saucy in the second logo embellished outfit.

Not many people dress up for this race, the odd fairy or superhero but generally club runners and happy locals raising money for their own charities or just for the fun of taking part. The race is supported by my old running club, Spa Striders, who pack the post-race goodie bags and provide most of the marshals so I knew I would see a familiar face or two en route but I am not sure that Anne was prepared for being launched into the spot light. Happy to support and stay in the shadows, the almost instantaneous attention from both the local press and fellow runners who wanted a pre-race selfie was a little overwhelming and felt sure she regretted donning the yellow outfit. No going back now Anne, so I think she just embraced the moment and went with it.

With the support of the great gang from Zero to Hero and old friends alike, a chance to catch up and more photos, we soon made our way to the start line and we were on our way.

The first half of the run is out of town around the local common/golf course so support was patchy once away from the start but heading back into town, the streets were lined and the support was overwhelming, we heard the usual cry's, "ketchup", "come on you saucy pair" but the best "look mummy, here come the condiments", That posh that and no more than I would expect from the Royal Borough.

My hometown looked stunning on this beautiful morning, blue skies and sunshine brought the best out in this lovely spa town and the final mile through the Jepson Gardens was stunning. I could hear the finish and yet more familiar faces, turning for home, I grabbed Anne's hand, let's do this. The cheers were deafening and crossing the finish line, we had left our mark.

Later in the day, as the organisers thanked everyone on Social Media, Anne and I's photo taken at the start of the race provided the backdrop, sorry Anne.

15th April 2018 - Phew!

What a week in the 56notout camp! I expected it to be busy, but I did not allow for transport issues adding into the mix, delaying a couple of challenges until next week.

If it wasn't busy enough as it was, the reshaping of my car's rear end potentially stopped one of my most dreaded challenges before it started, but I am happy to report that no one was hurt and unfortunately, we made it to Alton Towers!

Rollers Coasters bring many of my fears together , heights, speed, disorientation and control to name a few but having changed colour looking like my breakfast might make a reappearance, my fear of roller coasters was reaffirmed ,but on the positive side, it turned out to be a great 56notout family effort.

Once I had regained some colour in my cheeks, there was a guest appearance at the Ricoh Stadium and later on stage with the band Chain Of Fools, I feel good, and am glad that a few notes appeared from the trombone when I needed them to, but have been advised not to give up my day job..

Some great publicity for the challenge on the streets of my home town running The Regency run closed the first of a few busy last few weeks .

This time next week I will hopefully have completed at least 3 more challenges including a big one ,The London Marathon !, look out for the ketchup bottle if you're watching on the telly.

I am looking forward to the end of my 56 alcohol free days on Marathon day on Sunday, but it might be sensible to wait till AFTER the race is over I think..

A big thank you to Alton Towers, Wasps, Hamish and the Chain of Fools, Anne for being my mustard, Round Table and fellow runners along with the wonderful folks of Leamington for their continuing help and support.

THE BELLS, THE BELLS

I must confess, this is something I always wanted to try my hand at and thought, with at least one church in pretty much every village, town and city in the country, I would be spoilt for choice but as I have already eluded to, it's all about getting connected to the right person. Life moves in funny ways and surprised when several pleas for help resulted in the same person, so it was meant to be.

John Hammond bell captain at St. Leonard's Church, Ryton came to my rescue and arranged for me to join the bell ringers at one of the regular Monday night practice sessions. Arriving ahead of the main group, John gave me the tour of the beautiful 15 century tower although parts of the church dating back to 1080 AD and is one of the oldest Norman churches in Warwickshire and showed me the ropes (you knew I was going to say that at some point, didn't you?). I found the mechanics of the bell ringing process fascinating and so much more to it that I expected. Balancing above the bells, high up in the tower should have been a challenge on its own along with navigating the narrow staircase when at one point I regretted having that extra slice of pie and thought I might get stuck in the stair well but back in the comfort of the rope room, John showed me the basic technique. I never imagined that it would be so difficult mainly because the action did not reflect the sound output and seemed to be an unnatural process.

I also soon realised that get it wrong and the power of bell became apparent as the rope was wrenched from my hands nearly pulling my shoulder out of its socket. Like all new things, practice makes perfect but no training bells tonight with some taxing "on the job" training this was a great experience and a privilege to have a go at something on my bucket list in such a magnificent building.

I hope we didn't disturb the neighbours too much.

GOOD EVENING DERBY!

This challenge came out of the blue and surprisingly gave me "three bangs for my buck". The offer came from my nephew, Jaymie Icke, a great supporter of Shelter and my challenge year and provided a pretty obvious win from within in the family.

My older sister Linda was married to former professional footballer and television presenter David Icke. More well known for his famous announcement on the BBC's prime time show Wogan in 1991 that he had been told by a psychic that he was a son of the godhead. The appearance turning him from a respected household name into a victim of public ridicule. Starting his football career as goalkeeper for Coventry City, today he is a prolific author as a professional conspiracy theorist his controversial views selling out venues worldwide with his lectures although we don't mention David's past regarding playing for Coventry City ....

Today, David was speaking at Derby County Football ground to a capacity audience in the Pedigree Suite in the Pride Park Stadium promoting his new book "Everything you need to know, but have never been told" and pre show, Dave signed a copy - challenge number 37 "get a book signed by an author" - boom.

The tour was travelling up and down the country along with further afield to an ever growing following but David is not always welcome and attracts protesters as well as supporters so the location for many lectures a secret until just before the show to avoid any potential issues so arriving at Pride Park, I was told to follow the signs for the BT conference. Dave's shows are a real family affair with both my nephews, Jaymie and Gareth along with my sister involved in the smooth running of the event. Gareth, accomplished singer/songwriter provides the pre lecture entertainment and allowed me to take to the stage to kick off the night. I had to say it "Good evening Derby!" With no script or notes, I did my sales pitch and explained who I was and why I was in front of this eclectic group of people all captured on video for prosperity by Beth, Jaymie's fiancé. I loved it and felt confident and glad of this special opportunity thanks to David, Jaymie and the team.

Filled with a new sense of confidence I introduced Gareth to perform and headed off stage to round of applause. Thank you, Derby, and leaving whilst still light, I seized the moment and ran under the watchful eye of the statue of Sir Brian Clough, city number 7.

I'M A KNIGHT GET ME OUT OF HERE!

I really wanted to spend St George's Day dressed as a knight but decided to use a little poetic licence as I would be in London on the 23rd following the marathon so thought the Friday before would be a good idea. Not only would it encourage people to part with a pound or two just before the weekend and a half day to so morale is always better.

The marathon was always a good talking point and a challenge that a lot of people to aspire too and it's not every day you see a pretty good likeness of the patron saint of England walking around the office. The idea came from an old friend and colleague Steve Porter who ever since we met flew the flag for England and Saint George, unfortunately he has left IAC so will not get to see the outfit in the flesh but he was first to see the picture, once I had put the bins out much to the amusement of Julie, his response was typical Steve "that is fuckin ace".

I had to drop Millie off at school en route and the looks I was getting were funny and made the journey go a lot quicker. I parked a short walk from the office, enough to allow most of the office to see my arrival. I was delighted to escort Sophie Biddle into the building. The most perfect maid Marian I could have wished for and I regret not getting a picture but we looked the part, the knight and a damsel in distress - sadly, we parted at the door and the short walk to my desk was comical and a surprise to many.

After the initial reactions, it was business as normal, I had work to do and meetings to attend. Surprising how colleagues just accepted me and got on with it, the only difference was my bucket growing heavy as the morning went on, I took every opportunity to extract a coin or two from everyone and remind folks that I had a marathon to run at the forthcoming weekend.

The morning was punctuated with another challenge, a bit of fun and a chance to involve others, the current intake of apprentices to be precise. Made famous by hit tv show, I'm a celebrity get me out of here, we would be adapting the gruesome television challenge to some a little more user friendly especially as I had a few miles to run and did not need an upset tummy or even worse. Some great photos and a chance to see the less formal side of my nature and good fun too. Leanne, who helped me organise the support, still has to endure the taste roulette at home as I donated the jelly bean based game to her children, rotten fish and mouldy cheese not that appetising to be honest.

My boss, Kevin made me smile as I headed for home, "back to normal Monday, Kev" I said, "for you Mr Atherton, define normal" came his reply. Brilliant.

The next time I would enter the office, I would have completed the London marathon and maybe I would take the lift.

LONDON CALLING!

With less than 24 hours to go before I take on the 26.2 miles of the iconic London marathon. I took the opportunity to do an impromptu blog from my phone.

21st April 2018 - Let's do this

Be afraid folks, a rare blog from my phone without the excellent services of my editor who keeps be on the straight and narrow.

So today en route to London to join Team Shelter for the iconic London Marathon. After a busy few weeks with many challenges completed, meeting great people and a bit of fun too, it will be good to have a relax at the hotel before heading of to the start at Greenwich.

Thank you for all help and support, I am moved to tears at times but is giving me the energy to keep going.

Good luck to my fellow runners and see you on the other side :-)

Am I looking forward to a beer after, oh yes!!!

The emotions hadn't quite kicked in, but the following morning was a completely different story. I did not sleep that great and after a restless night, the reality of what was ahead had become all too real, standing in docklands on the morning of the marathon I was an emotional wreck. I failed miserably to hold back the tears and if I was going to add any more worry to the family, those 20 seconds in front of the camera did a pretty good job.

Travelling down the morning before with Richard, Sue and Annie Cox, the mission today was to collect our race numbers and stay off our feet as much as possible, very easy in the big smoke. The marathon expo is something else, a chance to stock up on freebies and the obligatory photo call in front of anything with the logo on but we were all keen to getting settled into our hotel and have a relax so numbers collected, photos taken and a few extra gels purchased (just in case) we headed to our hotel, only a couple of stops on the Docklands Light Railway to West India Quay in Canary Wharf.

Marathon fever had engulfed the Marriott Hotel and do not think there was a guest in the hotel that was either running or with someone that was. The staff had pulled out all the stops, every runner received a goody bag and the refreshing fruit punch a plenty. Once in my room, it was time to lay my kit out and maybe a little snooze.

Refreshed, we had a wonder around before dinner with a couple of alcohol-free beers then an early night after phoning home. Even with 12 hours before the start, my heart was racing, sleep did not come easily tonight I knew but as long as I could get some rest it would help.

Race day started with an early wake up call, a bit of fresh air and a post on social media before a healthy but filling breakfast. As my next meal would be sometime away so I made good choices, plenty of carbohydrates so I at least I would not start hungry.

After the marathon, we planned a hotel nearer the finish so having checked out, I had to carry all the extra goodies I had seemed to accumulate. Meeting Sue in reception, Richard and Annie would enjoy a lie in, my feelings of anxiety and apprehension went up another level. The threatened tube strike that had dominated the day's running up to marathon weekend had thankfully been resolved so we continued with plan A and as we walked the short distance to the D.L.R. station, Sue asked if I was ok. She already had noticed the change in my attitude, the outgoing devil may care Steve had been replaced with a very quiet person who I am not Sue had ever met before. I was looking inward and desperately trying to find some inner strength, I knew I had not put enough training in and with the warnings predicting one of the hottest London marathons on record and advising against costumes did not help my confidence in seeing the finish. The atmosphere on the train was electric, everyone was race ready and the air full of tension and the smell of deep heat. A very eclectic mix of runners, some looked like athletes, others Sunday joggers and everything in between. All ages and nationalities, each with the intent of crossing the finish line on the Mall. Arriving at Greenwich station, the tension spilled out onto the streets of the London suburb and the marathon circus had arrived in town.

As a rule, runners are good people and with a shared aim the camaraderie was infectious enhanced by helpful and smiling marshals with a clearly apparent police presence, a sign of this changing world we live in.

I was dressed as an average runner with my signature 56notout outfit quietly waiting in a bag ready to be launched on the world. Sue reminded me that, due to the high temperatures, I promised Julie that I would not wear the outfit but knew I would. Walking quietly with Sue through the leafy pathways of Blackheath Park, it was soon time to part as she headed off to the green start zone with the athletes and the red zone for me at the very back with the real folks as I like to call them. The charity plodders, rhinos, toilets, fairies and a chap with a karaoke machine. Once my rucksack dropped off at the line of baggage trucks, I had a little wonder around, still carrying the ketchup outfit poised ready to launch onto the world. It was only early in the morning, but already the sun was shining with the day already shaping up to be a hot one.

I took the opportunity to speak to fellow Shelter runners, clearly identified by the red t shirts with Shelter in big writing, not that difficult to be honest and at one of my many toilet visits, I was delighted to bump into the legendary Gary McKee. Exchanging a bit of banter with the promise of a run before the challenge year was over, we shook hands and I headed back to loiter around the holding area. This seemed to be the gathering point for the folks in fancy dress who had also decided to ignore the guidance from the organisers and go for it. One of the highlights of the morning was meeting Graham Burns, or "Karaoke Man" as he is better known, running for Breast cancer research. Entertaining fellow runners, I was delighted to see we were in the same start pen along with a huge beast and a panto dame. Feeling like I had known these folks for years, the time waiting to make our way to the start line was just the best, my nerves and thoughts of the 26.2 miles ahead put to the back of mind as we all sang the classic singalong songs spanning the decades.

I posted a video on social media to give flavour of what the atmosphere is like as the tension builds.

The next few hours were a blur to be honest, once we had crossed the start line and the tracking commenced so my followers knew I was on my way, finishing was inevitable, only the question was when. The support was legendary, the crowd shouted, clapped and offered an array of goodies. I felt great for the first few miles, passing iconic landmarks, canary wharf, the Cutty Sark, Greenwich and the memorable tower bridge marking half way, only 13 miles to go and with the early afternoon, came the threatened high temperatures and it was already getting pretty warm inside the ketchup outfit. I took on fluids at every opportunity along with odd roadside snack offered by spectators but with a desire to finish strong and conscious of my ability, I eased off the pace. Never short of support and an encouraging "Come on Steve" and the usual sauce related comments, I was delighted to see some familiar faces from Spa Striders, my old running club and David Chantrey captured my mood and would become a great lasting photographic memory of a great day but I had a few miles to run before I could celebrate. If you listen to the experts, running a marathon is all in the head, ok you need a good level of fitness and a good pair of trainers but the head fights you every single mile of the route and passing the half way point is a psychological land mark having run further than the miles remaining and a good feeling to be the right side of the Thames. Along the route, a regular feature of well organised events, a shower tunnel provided a cooling mist and dropping the outfit off, short shorts and a vest top gave a chance to drop my body temperature down a degree or two and helping the miles progress.

A heart-warming sight to see the London landmarks in the distance knowing that Big Ben marked the final run in to the finish outside Buckingham Palace, but still 10 miles or so to go. Running, like most activity is about breaking it down into manageable portions, the age-old question about how to eat an elephant, the answer, a bit at a time. Cheesy but true and does work although not a great fan of elephant but at around 20 miles, I could have eaten two. Another boost came at just after the 21-mile mark when I saw a great friend and fellow runner Harkey (one of my 56 runners too) and the fabulous support from Run Dem Crew, a community running group who run the streets of the capital. She ran down the road and flung her arms and legs around me, just magic and kept me going to the finish. I was in good spirits now, helped with single figures left to run so started to chat with the crowds as I slowly ran. any sigh of Mo, I asked.

The witty answers made me smile, no you got him licked, knowing full well that the Olympic legend Mo Farah had finished many hours before and by now would have showered, been fed and watered and catching up on the soaps no doubt. But this was my run, my challenge and in my head, it was all about me. Time was irrelevant, just about finishing and ticking off another challenge plus a city, London #8, along with the end of a dry period. Three bangs for the buck - not a bad day at the office.

Little did I know as I ran along the embankment towards Big Ben that the day had done so much more. I had my phone in airplane mode to save battery so with the last mile to go, I recorded my steady progression past the crowds in Whitehall and into Birdcage Walk and with Buckingham

Palace on my left, I took a sharp right and headed for the finish line on the Mall and the medal. The elation of crossing the finish line was immense and the sense of relief amazing.

With my baggage collected and with a smile on my face, I headed for the Rubens Hotel and the arms of my wife. By the time I left St James's Park I had called all the significant people in my life, delighted to hear the news that donations to the Shelter Just Giving page had passed the £2000 target, phew! and as I walked down Buckingham Palace Road, I could see Julie outside the Bag O Nails pub with a beer, the ketchup outfit was soaking wet and did not smell that great but it felt like one of the family, we had been through a lot but I was glad to take it off and feel the air on my body.

One amazing day and so glad to be the other side of the finish line and with the woman I love. Like the Marriott Hotel in docklands, the staff at Rubens had also taken the event to heart and walking into the hotel reception, albeit a little slowly, I felt like an A list celebrity especially when I was presented with my chocolate medal by the hotel staff.

After a shower and some food, more beers were consumed in the hotel bar as Julie and I shared our day. Being the nonrunner in a marathon team is as hard if not harder than running, this is Julie's side of the day -

Julie's thoughts on day

After months of training in the dark, rain, snow and just about anything else that could be thrown at him, the day had come.

I waved him off to London the day before, sounding like a stuck record,

" don't wear the ketchup outfit, it's crazy, you'll get heat stroke"

" be careful, walk if you have too"

"don't be a hero, just stop if it's too much "

All of the above I was confident he'd completely ignore.

I tried to enjoy a day of peace, stocking up on snacks to shovel down him if history repeated itself and he collapsed in a big heap at the end like last time, but that's another story.

I headed to London myself on the Sunday morning having endured attempting to watch two previous marathons I now know by learning the hard way that it is virtually impossible to be at the start, finish and somewhere in between without actually walking a marathon yourself,

the first time in London, with two reluctant smallish children in tow, and the second in 6 hours of pouring, freezing rain in Edinburgh, I think it's the spectators that should get the medal.

We'd decided the finish was the best bet.

On the train, I was constantly checking the very useful virgin app to see what was going on, interrupted constantly by messages from excited but anxious family

He'd started! It was the hottest day of the year and Virgin were telling people not to wear costumes, but this is Steve we're talking about and he would definitely have it on, I was not happy.

I checked into the rather swanky Rubens hotel, although the luxurious room was tiny. I think I could touch all the walls at once, but that's London for you! I put on my Shelter T-shirt and headed out into the madness, London was buzzing and putting on a great show.

I found somewhere to get a drink, no chance of food, everywhere was heaving with spectators so I sat on a wall and attempted to make a meal of a bag of nuts.

My phone continued, the app is so clever it knows if the runner isn't moving, frantic texts

" why's he stopped? "

"What's he doing? "

"Is he ok? "

How the #*!*# do I know !

Visions of paramedics and ambulances

(which could constantly be heard) in my mind when in reality he was probably talking to people or taking selfies or maybe just having a pee!

It was a LONG day..

The estimated finish time approached and I found a spot to wait outside a pub near the hotel, experience has taught me that finding someone at the finish is impossible in an event that big, and obviously sitting with a drink is far more appealing and hey, I deserved it!

The little icon appeared, FINISHED !!!!

My phone lit up, so many people calling to tell me , I KNOW !!!
Plenty of tears of relief from everyone but mainly me,
I ordered the biggest beer I could get, this would be the first for Steve in 56 days, the end of another challenge of 56 alcohol free days.

After what seemed like forever, YES, I could make out that Ketchup bottle coming down Buckingham Palace Road like a celebrity , tears from both of us , that costume was not nice to be next to, but I didn't care, he'd made it and I was so proud of him, I may have shouted at him not to ever do it again !

That pint didn't touch the sides...

RUN #53 – KIRSTIE SMITH

I wasn't sure if running so soon after the London Marathon was such a good idea but have had a few days out I of the trainers, I thought that I was ready to pound the streets again. Kirstie, reporter at the local newspaper had been a great supporter of the challenge year from the start, always happy to find a space to tell the world what this crazy middle aged man was up to this week and more importantly keeping the issues surrounding homelessness under the noses of those who care and want to make a difference. Although Kirstie works in Leamington for Johnston Press PLC, the current owners of local weekly newspapers, the Leamington Courier, Warwick Courier and Kenilworth Weekly News, home is in the Cotswolds which is a good commute each day.

Conscious of Kirstie's drive home, we planned to meet outside the newsroom. A far cry from the images of old, smoke filled offices with the clatter of typewriters and ringing landlines. All very calm and high tech, laptops and internet, the tools of the trade these days although I image just occasionally someone does shout - "Hold the front page!". I am happy to take my place in the middle pages away from the headlines which usual is reserved for serious topics. The paper, with its localised titles always each derivative to be slightly tailored for each town but with a common content in all which generally saw the progress reports of my 56notout journey making it into all three publications.

This will not be the last you will hear about Kirstie, as we ran we talked about her own journey inspired by my own challenge year as she was about to embark on a series of tasks of her own, I guess these are those ripples that Nicola mentioned on our run.....

Run #54 – Phil Houghton

I like Phil and happy that we had the chance to run together as part of the challenge. Our paths have been crossing for many years, but this is the first time we have actually ran side by side together and actually had a conversation. Phil is one of life's "doers" and is always in the thick of the action, a real go to person and someone that I would always want on my team. Working in some "me time" for himself in life's busy schedule of the endless bookings for dads' taxi service which felt oh so familiar, I was pleased that after a bit of shuffling, the time and location for a run together was in the diary. Making excellent use of the time between drop off at scouts and the next pick up from theatre group or whatever was in the plan, Phil actively manages to get the preverbal "quart in a pint pot", so easy to sit in the car any loose hours in the virtual world of social media but from my own experience, this great use of the time between stuff is the best and a good feeling. Phil and I have so many mutual friends, manly running based but we also work in the same crazy industry, so the conversation flowed. It was good to run in Kenilworth on such a lovely evening and nice when I could sit back and enjoy the journey with someone else in the driving seat. Thanks Phil

NO NOT WATER AGAIN!

This challenge year has been all about pushing the boundaries and whenever water is involved, my heart rate increases. You already know that I am not a confident swimmer so a challenge that might involve me getting wet or even worse, end up in the river was never going to be very popular but as I get reminded constantly, this is not about having fun. I understand that safety needs to be considered when try something new, so when Tess, old friend and runner #51 invited me to join Royal Leamington Spa Canoe Club for one of their taster sessions.

I was born on the banks of the river Leam so was good to take to the water very close to my old home. I was nervous but knew I was in safe hands and amongst other trying something new I soon felt more relaxed. The fun started even before I ventured on to the water, trying a canoe for size in the boathouse I got cramp and had to be helped out of the boat to try to stretch my muscles and stop the pain. I was panicking, what would I do if this happened on the water. I was going in I was convinced but once on the water and we started to paddle into town I felt better. Getting the canoe to go in a straight line was not as easy as I thought, it become all about physics, centre of gravity and balance. I'm sure the boat had a mind of its own, but I was not going to beaten. Many times during the year, coaches and those experts who are at the top of their game use mind games to get the best out of people.

Up to now, the night was all about me trying to control the canoe but for this to work I had to be at one with the fibre glass beast so the instructors introduced games to give my brain something else to concentrate on and instantly became not about the boat - very clever. Once I started to feel the force, the control came with it. A very enjoyable evening and although I was pretty wet, I managed to not go into the river. Getting out was another kettle of fish, I am so glad that most of my fellow newbies had already headed into the club house and was relieved that my ungraceful exit from the canoe went largely unnoticed. I think I am getting the hang of water but only time will tell.

RUN #55 – SOPHIE WINDSOR

The timing for today's run was perfect in many ways and ever so slightly surreal. Sophie or Miss Windsor who I had known her as for many years in the role of being my daughters' PE teacher so was strange to be on first name terms after all these years. The girls loved Miss Windsor, firm but fair and full of life and was so pleased to get to know her a little more away from the school and also get the view of my kids from the other side of the table. A fellow marathon runner although much fitter than I'll ever be, sport of any kind is clearly her passion but playing the game and good sportsmanship the core values of her mindset and clearly runs off on the girls she teaches.

As we ran, we touch on school life, my daughters and the path that brought us together but today we talked about a broad spectrum of subjects and boy did we laugh. Taking in the sights of Leamington on a lovely late spring evening, I took the opportunity to chat to Sophie about my forthcoming visit to as the first in what I hoped to be the first of many school assemblies as I planned to take the challenge idea to schools and organisations, predictably called "56notout on tour". She was already ahead of the game and planned to line up some tame pupils to help me if I need any audience participation, so I felt happy that I had some welcome support when the time came.

THE ONES THAT GOT AWAY

Just like the classic fisherman's tall, some challenges never saw the light of day, some nearly happened but come to the day of the race, didn't come to fruition.

Tesco's had been really supportive throughout the year and when Helen from the Southam store introduced me to Melissa Hazell at the Warwick shop, I thought I might just end up doing something wacky on my doorstep. When Mel and I met, the idea of sitting in a bath of beans jumped out of nowhere. We knew that this might just take a bit of thinking about. The whole food waste issue soon came to the surface, I know that Tesco have real strict policies on food going to waste. I had to do some research with the help of Mel. Tesco were already working local to help the community, I went on to learn that ideally as a store they would like to have charities and organisations on board for every night of the week, daily they estimate how many trays of food aren't likely to be sold by a certain time , they then text that charity telling them how many trays of food we have and what it is i.e., produce, bakery or fresh they then reply to the text saying yes or no if they want it, if they say yes that's great the volunteer comes in and collects it. If it's not what the charity need at that time, i.e. trays full of say bakery products that they wouldn't use, they would say no in which case the goods would then be offered to another charity and so the process continues. If, after this process of offering to the other charities results in none of them want what is on offer, then the goodies would go to the next process, which is colleague shop then if the staff leave anything, what is left goes to the next stage which is animal feed. After that stage it goes towards energy.

STEVE ATHERTON

In a nutshell, first - charities, then staff followed by animals and finally energy. It was good to see that landfill is not one of the options. With this in mind, we tweaked the idea replacing beans with green gunk and also to keep me out of the paper and prison, I planned to where my trisuit along with a bath cap to add to the humiliation and keep what was left of my dignity in tacked.

I was ready, but on the day, the logistics of setting up a bath of gunk in the foyer of a busy supermarket became just a little bit of a big ask. Maybe this idea might make a future list, if and when I ever take on something like this again. I wasn't that disappointed to be honest; I was never really convinced that my hometown of Warwick was ready to see any more of my naked flesh and reckoned that it had seen more than enough already.

6th May 2018 - Time to reflect

Enough to put you off your BBQ, who needs a London Marathon medal to remind me of that amazing day better than a selection of black toes :-)

As I enter the last few weeks of my incredible year and the last push to complete the remaining challenges, the pressure is on. Most of the remaining items on the list are in the diary but a couple still need to be firmed up but I have faith that all will come good.

Seeing the good that is happening around me is brilliant and as I begin to the 56notout tour, ok I am talking at a school assembly but hopefully first of many chances to spread the word it gives me chance to look back on what has happened and also look ahead to the next chapter. No plans for 57notout but watch this space. The challenge maybe nearly over but the story continues ....

I still plan to keep running until the end of May, so please let me know if you fancy joining me for a trot and any clubs or societies who fancy a speaker. I can tailor the talk to the group.

Enjoy rest of the bank holiday folks and thank you for all your support. X

56NOTOUT ON TOUR

Something I wanted to do and was originally on the list as one of the challenges was to talk to a school assembly. Dropped from the plan in one of the early idea "culls" but I thought the PR would be a good experience and help develop my public speaking skills.

My appearance was on home turf, planning to speak at the whole school assembly at Kingsley. The school that both of my daughters attended and where I served as chair of the PTA or the Friends of Kingsley (or the "FoKers" as we were occasional called) for many years but walking out in front of nearly 300 pupils and teachers including my youngest daughter was still nerve racking nevertheless. I opted for a combination of a good old PowerPoint presentation with a smidgen of animation, courtesy of my youngest Millie together with some ad-lib dialogue with the occasional spot of audience participation. The school had kindly provided me with a nice lectern with amplification and everything but to be honest, I liked the freedom to walk around without the restriction of a microphone, moving my arms like a windmill at time but allowing me to get the message across, so I did feel very natural and at ease with my audience.

From the rousing round of applause once I closed my I maiden presentation, I felt like it had gone ok and was very much appreciated. I tried to combine some learning and hopefully thought-provoking words that might just resonate in the future maybe but also gave me a chance to look inside myself.

What have I learnt from the challenge year?

You have got to have a plan, if you don't know where you are going, any road takes you there.

I wish I had had a better plan.

I wish I had started planning earlier.

I soon realised that on the top of my to do list is not always top of others. What is important to me is not the same for other people, I had to be patient.

Need to adapt, not every egg is a bird.

If you want something- ask!

I hoped that if I sowed a seed somewhere in just one person's mind during that short assembly, then I would be happy but I will never know and in many ways, I like that, those ripples again.

Run #56 – Guy Jackson

Challenge complete but is it over?

One of favourite challenges and probably the one that I was so glad I had on the list was to run with 56 difference people. A challenge that I knew would take me most of the year to complete worth every mile in the trainers and had the added benefit of providing me with many new friends. Today's run with Guy Jackson was as special for him as it was me. We first met back in 2011 when we were on opposite sides of the same game or I was the supplier or worked for the supplier and Guy the customer working on a new vehicle launch for Jaguar Land Rover. Very quickly realising that working together, we could both make progress and keep everyone happy. Playing it straight and professional together with a bit of humanity and dignity, sometimes lacking in the car industry of recent years, we kept in touch via social media and the occasional phone call. I had Guy on my list pretty much on my list from day one but took the best part of a year to get something in the diary and a pure coincidence that he turned out to be number 56. The timing was perfect as Guy was about to commence on a journey of his own having just bought a canal side property very much in need of some TLC. So, a run along the Grand Union canal and past his new home was fitting and on such a lovely evening, a real treat.

I left the news that Guy was number 56 and the completion of another challenge until we started to record the now traditional video and I could tell he was thrilled. Challenge done but I still had more people on my list so I would carry on until the end and after all, I hadn't ran with Daniel Craig.

RUN #57 – GARY MCKEE

Who needs Daniel Craig anyway, I had the chance to run with the legend that is Gary McKee. Gary and I first met just before the challenge year started and his great advice has stood me in good stead as I ticked off the challenges. Our paths have crossed a few times during the past few months and I was keen to have Gary as one of my runners. Gary was in the Royal Borough for one of his famous fund-raising talks. Catherine and John will be hosting the soiree at their beautiful home later that day. Meeting at the Old Dairy, I had a chance to show Gary around my hometown.

Taking the morning off work, I was blessed with a stunning day with blue skies and sunshine making Leamington look at its best. It was good to get to know Gary and fill the gaps in the stories he tells at his talks, I like the detail. A word I love is passion and I love hearing his stories and the passion that oozes out of every sentence. I loved the way he talks of his family and during our run, I hear about his boys Beau aged 10 and Alfie two years old who originally planned to run every day of January following in their dads' footsteps raising money for Macmillan but they got carried away and Run January turned into run 2018. Gary was so proud of his lads, I thought he was going to explode he was so proud. Nearly twelve months since we first met, Gary's advice has been invaluable and grateful that the help keeps coming.

In the early days of the challenge, I approached several big companies looking for help and support, but I was too vague with my requests. I learnt that I had to be specific and clear, also I was a nobody, just a middle aged man with some wacky ideas, Gary assured me that I now had credibility and a proven track record on my CV so next time it would be easier, trust me, Gary added. Returning to the Old Dairy, preparation was already in full flight for the evening ahead, so after the now routine video, I head off to the office.

"The world needs more people like you Steve" were Gary's parting words......

Run #58 – Alex Everard

Alex had been on my 56notout journey, pretty much from the start. I recall discussing the idea with him running along the seafront at Roker, the seaside town just outside of Sunderland on one of our numerous visits to the north east of England, carrying out training with one of the manufacturing plants. The long drive usually spawned deep and meaningful conversation to a heavy rock soundtrack from the cars hard drive. Must have made a funny sight for passing cars had we sang along to Iron Maiden and such rock gods - very Wayne's World. No music as we ran today but good conversation and gave me a chance to see Alex's new home, the self-build project that has been keeping him entertained for the last few months plus provided somewhere new to run.

The guided tour of the new pad and a nice cuppa would have to wait until after our run, so with something to look forward to we headed out into the countryside and towards Walton Hall, the former home of flamboyant entertainer Danny La Rue, now a fancy hotel. The quiet lanes on the approach to the 16th-century country mansion in Walton, a small hamlet on the outskirts of Wellesbourne, provided a suitable spot for a comfort break with Alex warning me of the perils of stinging nettles. I won't mention the old joke about taking away the pain but keeping the swelling.

Alex has been a great support during the challenge year and his generosity has been really helpful and rallying the interest especially on the waxing challenge where his suggestion of extra areas of hair increased the traffic on social media. As for the now traditional run video, what can I say, the hits on Facebook were one of the highest during the year with followers enjoying the banter between the two of us and became one of my own highlights from the year. Returning to Chez Everard, the promised guided tour and a cuppa.

Good fun and good company, how far did we go, no idea and to be honest, neither of us gave a monkeys.

CATCHING A CRAB

Back on the water and this was another challenge that was given to be back in September 2017 when Kate Evans, a long-time running buddy and once fellow Strider ran together. During our run back in the autumn, we had to make a diversion to the boat house at Warwick Boat Club to pick up a sweatshirt. On the banks of river Avon in the shadow of the magnificent Warwick castle, Kate gave me the challenge along with the offer to make it happen. I had never actual been into the club grounds before then and I was overwhelmed by the location.

This was one challenge seemed to take an awful lot of effort to make happen and so grateful that Kate persevered with getting me on the water. Rowing is one of these things that done properly, looks so easy but I would soon realise that this was far from the case. I felt out of my comfort zone surrounded by very experienced rowers but to help me, Kate had enlisted her friend Jo and I was soon introduced to "the tub", a less than sleek boat as the name suggests which was reserved for beginners as it was a little more forgiving in the water which would hopefully mean I would stay out on the river. With "the tub" off the bank and into the water, the first challenge was to get aboard and into my seat. It may sound a little naive but even though I had used a rowing machine many times in the gym, I hadn't clocked the fact that your backside travelled up and down the boat on rails. Not sure why that obvious fact passed me by, but it did, every day is a school day.

Kate was the cox, keeping "the tub" on the straight and narrow whist leaving Jo and I doing all the hard work. More "on the job" training which continued to be the norm during my challenge year as Kate gave me a crash course in the rudiments of rowing. I had already been warned about "catching a crab" which is when the rows go out of sync and you risk getting a mouthful of oar, so I was going to listen and learn watching Jo's technique and rhythm.

I was having a ball, when I got in the sync with Jo, the tub glided through the water like a knife through butter and not unlike my canoe experience, it was all about feeling the process and not to think too hard. Being so close to the castle was a pleasure and I felt blessed as they say in Facebookland, lucky to live in a beautiful part of the world and grateful for good friends supporting me in my map cap challenge year. Completely immersed in the new experience, I neglected to take note of the blood running down my calves having carved a crimson hole in the back of my legs with every stroke. oh yes, maybe we should have got you some calf guards, Kate remarked. I didn't care, this was just a great experience and on the river at the bottom of our garden.

Making the short walk home through the park, I had a smile on my face from ear to ear, there was no mistake that I was having a ball.

A great challenge reminding me that working as a team, the output is greater than the sum of the individual components - profound stuff.

For most weeks, I would have been happy to tick off one challenge but with the end of the year in sight, I was pleased that after a bite to eat, I would be off to take on another challenge in the same day and the next one could not have been more different.

GETTING DIRTY

If you want something just ask! I first met Peter back in November at Warwick's annual Victorian evening and Christmas light switch on. The atmosphere was enhanced by the authentic smell of a steam traction engine along with aroma of roasting chestnuts so I thought I would seize the moment and take five minutes to do my sales pitch. Peter without hesitation, was happy to help, we exchanged numbers and email addresses, but the English climate was having its part to play, and I would have to wait until the better weather. Time was of the essence and keep the focus on making this challenge happen as it was the only one that had anything with four wheels albeit cast iron and fuelled by coal, but I loved the nostalgia associated with steam. When it came to the day, Peter could not be around but he made all the arrangements and assured me that if I headed to the site of a company working in the construction industry in Astwood Bank and asked for Joe Norris it would all be sorted and I could get to drive something steam powered. I had Millie for company and moral support which also gave her a chance to experience a mode of transport that did not have a USB port or any hi-tech gadgets.

As soon as we turned off the main road onto the company's premises, we knew we were in the right place. There were traction engines everywhere heading in every direct much to the dislike of Millie. These machines are huge and not fitted with ABS or parking sensors and with my limited knowledge of traction engines, I know they weight a ton and do not stop in a hurry.

Joe Norris from the National Traction Engine Trust and his team were very obligingly and soon had me at the wheel of a fine specimen from the factory of John Fowler & Co of Leeds for a lap of the yard. I didn't realise that driving these mechanical beasts can be a two-man job, one to control the power and the other the direction. Nothing about anything steam engines is clean as both Millie and I soon found out, she only took photographs and still ended up with black hands. Driving the traction engine lack any sort of refinement and not unlike the tank, was all about brute force, no sign of power steering on this machine. Turning was a full body work out all on its own and if I spent any longer at the wheel, I might be able to cancel my gym membership.

Another great challenge completed and another lesson in how hard simple things can be when you do have the support of technology to take away the effort.

RUN #59 – LIBBY ATHERTON, CITY #9 – LEEDS

To be given the chance to run in a city, number #9, with only one to go and another runner plus the final outing of the ketchup bottle, I knew this was always going to be epic day and a one to remember, a significant city and a very special runner by my side. The runner today was my first born, Libby, the literary member of the family, I thought I would let her tell you in her own words her account of the day. The significance of Leeds, I let Libby tell you.

Leeds half marathon – Mustard madness

Leeds will always have a special place in my heart- it's where I spent three years of University, learnt how to use a washing machine, got engaged and finally discovered that Bob Marley is actually dead. Sad but true, Tim says I'm the thickest clever person he's ever met, and I think he's definitely onto something there.

Therefore, it made perfect sense for Leeds to be my 56 Not Out run location. I'd always bragged on the phone to Dad about the gorgeous runs I'd been on in Leeds, through stunning Roundhay park and down breath-taking country trails. So naturally, Leeds Half Marathon was the best opportunity to show him what all the fuss was about again in our second Leeds Half Marathon.

First time round, I still lived in Leeds however this time, Tim and I travelled up the day before for a nice getaway to our favourite city. Whilst Dad met us on race morning for a juicy bowl of porridge to get us ready for the big day.

We said our farewells to Tim and headed on down to Victoria Square in full costume, getting numerous confused looks as we passed copious Uni students nursing last night's epics in town. Spicy Mustard and Ketchup were back again!

As we arrived in the square to begin our half marathon warm up, we caught the attention of Radio Aire, a home grown Leeds radio station that I used to pass regularly on my trips around Leeds the previous year. They took some photos and gave us a shout out, catching the attention of fellow runners who thought us crazy, being one of the few people dressed up on a very toasty Sunday morning!

The run was tough, I'm not going to lie, especially with abundant inclines and some inexorable straight roads. But, as with every race, it's the supporters that get you through! The cheering, singing, Jelly Babies and admiration for the distance and the incredible people running around you is phenomenal.

Dad and I always call Leeds Half, the Aldi run because we start the race running past the Aldi, I shopped in during my first year and end the run passing the Aldi I shopped in in my final year. Sounds silly but knowing how far away we are from that end Aldi is reassuring for me and knowing that the 13.1 miles are almost over is both comforting but is bittersweet, because you know that the laughs, jokes and cheering is nearly over.

I absolutely love races, especially races that end with a pint of beer - albeit alcohol free! They are always very emotional for me, as I am always in complete admiration that my body manages to slog it round the 13.1 miles and seeing all the crowds cheering your name at the end is enough to bring a tear to my eye. Especially when I'm running with such an incredible person and for such an amazing cause!

13th May 2018 - Any sauce

Today is Sunday so must be Leeds and they did us proud!!! The support was amazing and saw the ketchup and mustard outfits final outing and what a great job they have done. Loads of media attention again but the big red one is ready for a wash - it stinks but I have run over 100k in it!

I am not sure what way is up, the last few challenges in the diary (well most of them but I am not panicking just yet) and glad to put my feet up at the end of another busy week.

I appreciate has helped and coming to my result with many of my strange requests. I still need to do some fire breathing and if anyone is wondering, I have had a couple of attempts on the unicycle but I think it's my fear of heights that is not helping although only two feet off the ground, I will keep trying.

Thanks all for sticking with me :-)

Hang on to your hats!

What happen in the next 48 hours was a blur and I was going to need a good night's sleep and a full English if I was going to stand any chance of lasting the distance. This would be one of the many "super weekends" of the 56notout year and by the end of it, I would have completed four challenges and ran with another three people. With the end of the final month well underway I had to take the pace up a notch or two.

RUN #60 – PHIL MANCELL

Signing off from the office, the first challenge on the list was to run with my old buddy Phil Mancell. Phil was a pup when we first met, taking him under my wing when he joined the team is now running teams of his own but although both busy, still make time for a chat and the occasional beer. I wanted to run with Phil, since we met back in February 1995 we have always got on, always knew what to order for me from "Wobbly Bobs", the local café, and at times spending more time together than with our families, we have both had some bumpy sections on life's journey. We ran, we talked, we laughed, reminiscing about life characters that seem to be missing from today's working lives. Jack the hat, Fat Wallet, Bush baby, the Rottweiler, the list is endless - these names were engineers, draughtsman but with history and a past that gave them there pseudonyms and were legends in their own lifetimes. Some no longer with us, gone to the great job shop in the sky but others still earning a crust in this crazy industry of ours. We had fun and I think Phil thought it would be all about the run and instead it was all about life.

Ride a Harley Davidson

I cannot believe it took nearly a year to bring this challenge home with so many times I thought it was in the bag and then complications and diary clashes. At one point, I thought I could combine this challenge with another and maybe arriving in style on the back of the iconic Hog, but Steve and Janice Harvey came to the rescue. I have never ridden a motorcycle in anger opting for the comfort of four wheels when it was time for me to take to the road but I have been a pillion many times but the older I get the more nervous passenger I have become regardless of the mode of transport.

Climbing on the back of Steve's XL 1200 R Sportster for the technophobes amongst the readers, I did everything I could to hide my fear. Steve asked if I had been on the back of a bike before. I was honest, yes but a long time ago and I will be a very nervous passenger. I must say Steve was a gentleman, rather than dismissing my fears, but taking in steady. We rode to a nearby village where Janice was ready to capture the event on camera. When Steve spotted his other half, he blimp the throttle and my heart rate did the same.

By the time we returned to Leamington, I had relaxed a little, but Steve was very astute." I can see what the significance of this challenge is for you Steve, you are a control freak and hate not being in the driving seat." He was right of course; I hate handing over the reins and allow another call the shots.

IF CARLSBERG DID BIKE RIDES

As the advertisement campaign launched in the seventies for that well-known Danish Euro fizz announced, if Carlsberg did bike ride this would be the one. The original plan was to cycle 100 miles from London to Leamington, a distance that had been in sight but never achieved but so far into the challenge year, I didn't have the legs for such a distance so opted to have a memorable ride with a great bunch of lads. I put the word out and I was inundated with riders wanting to join me along with numerous offers of help too, so was easy to bring this challenge home.

I picked a date, but little did I know at the time Prince Harry and Megan would choose the same day to get married. I thought people would drop out but to my surprise and delight the numbers keep on growing. Great friend and avid cyclist, Phil Bowser offered to lead the peloton and had a lovely route in mind with a breakfast stop on route and a beer at the end. Leaving home, one became two at the end of my road meeting Paddy, together we cycled to Kenilworth where two became ten meeting Mark, Phil, two Ian's, Matt and another three Steve's. By the time we reached our start point, the symbolic Coventry Cathedral were 13 strong with the addition of Nigel, Paul and Rob.

Phil gave the assembled group some words of wisdom before we headed out on the quiet streets of Coventry on retracing our tracks back through Kenilworth and out through Hatton and on to Alcester. The Cow Shed at the Yew Tree Garden Centre in Wootton Wawen provided the perfect venue for breakfast. The route was stunning, and the natural rotation of the group ensured that by the end of the 95km we were a team and a beer or two in the garden of the

Millwright Arms was the perfect end to a perfect morning. We might have been in the minority with most of the country watching probably the last Royal Wedding in my lifetime, but we had an amazing time and as the famous slogan goes "If Carlsberg did bike rides .... - you know the rest"

Thanks Gents, it was a pleasure riding with you.

WHAT A DAY!

I had a pretty easy day yesterday with only one challenge although I did spend a good few hours in the saddle but today, Sunday should be the day of rest according to the good book but I did not see that happening any time soon as I headed off to aptly named "Get Stuffed" Cafe in Ball Hill, Coventry to meet Paul and the rest of Bedworth Saints Scooter Club.

Even though I know plenty of people with scooters, it was my old mucker Stevie P that came to rescue and put me in touch with Paul Marshall who was going to do the honours but life had other ideas and a call from him just after I had arrived put the kibosh on the plan having broken down on route with what sounded like a pretty terminal mechanical problem as was waiting for a tow truck to arrive to return him and the ailing scooter back home.

I had already told 56notout story to Kirstie, Stuart and the rest of the scooter fanatics from the Saints and thinking that I was going to be out of luck but without hesitation, Stuart stepped up to the plate and with the loan of a helmet and jacket, looking every bit the part, I was travelling down the Walsgrave Road on my very own mini scoot ride out.

The offer of gloves did make me smile when I questioned the need as it was a warm late spring day. No, it's in case you fall off. I had no intention of falling off but appreciate the concern. The ride was great and with a smile on my face, I headed off to the second challenge of the day.

Run #61 – Michelle Dunn

Having said my thanks and goodbyes to "the Saints", I returned to the familiar configuration of four wheels and drive the short distance to the Memorial Park to meet runner number 61, Michelle Dunn. Michelle had already helped with a previous challenge to try my hand at Acro-yoga and we agreed to get a run in before the challenge year was over and to have a catch up. Cabin crew for that well-known British airline, I enjoy hearing her stories from around the world but usually it's about her love life and her ability to attract the wrong sort of man. I told her that she needed a nice chap in her life but was straight back at me in her northern accent – "the nice ones are boring Steve; I want a bit of excitement". I couldn't fault her sentiment but from experience the two rarely go together. The park had a buzz about it and would be home to the BBC biggest weekend at the end of the month and the conversation from park to festival site was in full swing with the stage emerging above the temporary perimeter fence. Even though the event would take over a large part of park, the 48.5-hectare site had more than enough space for everyone today. The Memorial Park was opened in July 1921 as a tribute to the 2,587 Coventrians who died between 1914 and 1918 fighting in the First World War. Coventry Council bought the land from the Lords of Styvechale Manor, the Gregory-Hood family, when it was little more than a large grassed area that once formed Styvechale common. Heading away from the concert venue, the shady tree lined avenues provided a pleasant route for our catch up on this beautiful May morning. Stopping mid run at the foot of the 90 foot high war memorial monument to take some photos and record the infamous video, Michelle wanted to add a fitting twist and promptly dropped to the floor and did a hand stand making the resulting video very different, not every day I chat to someone upside down.

Dare to be different, I like that.

What's next asked the man?

Taking time to catch my breath, I grabbed a coffee and sat and watched the world go by until the final challenge of the day. Something I had never done before and one I was looking forward to, a colour run or a Colour Blast Dash to give today's event it's official title and I didn't have to leave the Memorial Park to join the fun. Some of the many things I have done over the last few months, I have been on my own and on occasion I had some company but for today's challenge, I was delighted to have my youngest daughter Millie with me. I should have counted this twice as to get her out for a run was a challenge in itself. Millie does not do sport, once describing running as the "sport of the devil". I always wanted to do a challenge together and we came up with doing a colour run.

Run #62 – Colour blast dash with Millie Atherton

Millie takes JIT or "just in time" to a new level, I like being ready, on time and in control. As for my baby, never late but only just. I was prepared, numbers, T shirts and paint, on the start line, I had done all the pre run stuff and I was ready for both of us so I chattered to Jane and Kathy from Zero to Hero. We had done the pre start mayhem, just to make sure no one starts in a clean white T shirt. "On my way" came the text, I was on the start line as Millie wondered up, put on her T shirt and off we went, getting our first dusting of fluorescent powder, pink if my memory serves me correct as we crossed the start line and I began the circuit of the memorial park for the second time that day. The difference being that this time we were periodically doused in brightly coloured paint. I had never done anything like this in my life. Millie enjoyed the paint stations but would be first to admit that she wasn't a big fan of the running part of in between but I was delighted to have her by my side and hand in hand we crossed the finish line getting another dusting for good measure. I don't think any part of our bodies escaped the intrusion of the powder paint and Millie was off into town, will Megs car ever going to recover from a colour blast dashed Millie?

What a day!

20th May 2018 - The end is in sight

Apologies for a bit of duplication but ....
   What an amazing 48 hours in the 56notout camp!

With less than 2 weeks to go, the pressure is on. This weekend as with the rest of the year, I have had the pleasure to meet some fabulous people who have go out of their way to help me.

Phil, Michelle and Millie that have added to the every growing list of runners that I have be delighted to spend time with.

Thankyou to Janice and Steve for getting me out in the back of a Harley and Paul, Kirstie and Stuart from Bedworth Saints for a mini scooter ride out.

The Carlsberg bike ride with Paddy, Nigel, Steve's, Rob, Mark, Paul, Ian, Matt, Richard and of course Phil for keeping the peloton together through the stunning lanes of our beautiful country.

Millie, Jane and Kathy for getting blasted in paint with me at the Colour Blast Dash in Coventry.

Whist I was doing all that , Emma, Iain, Faye and Julie we all hard at work preparing for Birmingham Pride and Libby getting my pole all shining ready for Wednesday's attempt at a bit of dancing.

And I still cannot that unicycle !!!!

Be a DJ

My third and final visit to the studios of BBC Coventry and Warwickshire, the local radio station was planned as closure to the challenge year and PR rather than a challenge. I love the atmosphere of the radio station, calm yet efficient but always exciting. What a great place to work I always think, regretting that I should have explored more career options when I was younger - hindsight and all that. Today I would be meeting weekday morning show presenter Vic Minett. After the usual formalities with the production team, I grabbed a coffee and sat and watched the radio station going about the business of entertaining the good folks of Warwickshire.

I sat in ore as the team made the production look effortless, a skill itself as I can only imagine the planning and expertise that goes into making it look so easy. Before long I was heading into the studio to meet Vic, what a lovely person and felt immediately at ease. As the music played and Vic and I chatted "off air" aware of some knob fiddling going on as my voice levels were being adjusted in anticipation of being broadcast live to the outside world. Soon I was "on air" and telling the world about my amazing year, I was getting good at this at last. I knew what I wanted to say and the important stuff that needed to be mentioned, Facebook pages et al. Lessons learnt from previous radio appearances, every day really is a school day.

Vic enquired if I had all the challenges ready and I said I was still missing one. Quick as a flash, I was yet again having some on the job training. Sat in the driving seat, Vic challenged me to introduce a song life on air, no pressure then. The song was "there she goes" by the La's and as

I played at being a DJ, another challenge off the list unfortunately I missed a golden opportunity to dedicate the song to Julie.

Maybe I shouldn't give up my day job.

As the challenge year entered the final straight heading towards the finish line, I didn't know which way was up and neither did the family. I was in and out of home with Julie or I never quite sure what I was going to do next. When asked my movements for the next day, my reply often brought raised eyebrows and a look of shock together with a tinge of inevitability. "What is it tonight Steve?" "Pole dancing with Libby, shouldn't be too long". Sent on my way with a "Ok baby, take care".

Am I getting that predicable and the is the extraordinary becoming the norm?

GOING UP THE POLE

And so, I was off to try my hand at pole dancing. Libby was an expert and even has her own pole in her kitchen. Once the accessory of choice at many a gentleman's establishment across the world, the simple pole once only associated with pole dancing has been reinvented and is now a piece of respectable sports equipment and pole dancing has become vertical fitness. Arriving at FPS Fitness in Yardley Wood, I was not sure what to expect. Is this a woman only thing or is it something lads do as well?

I had my own thoughts and I guess some preconceptions of what a vertical fitness studio would look like and the type of people who would attend. I knew it would not be easy, I have been told about pole dancing and can see, sorry been told that it is not as easy as it looks. Flexibility, coordination and upper body strength I would soon learn are key prerequisites that I would need if I stood any chance of not looking a complete spoon. Being just shy of sixteen stone would not help either. I was way out of my comfort zone. As I expected, I was the only male, surrounded by fit young ladies, a third of my age and half my weight but the warm and support was apparent from the start. I was made so welcome and whist Lisa guided everyone through some basic moves, Libby was on hand with one to one tuition for her old dad.

The others seemed to have grasped the basics but the engineer in me was working overdrive. This pole was never going to stay upright with a middle-aged man going throwing himself at this free standing eight-foot-tall shiny rotating chrome thing, it was going to end in tears. For this to happen, I had to put my trust in the equipment and most of all put complete faith in myself, the later was the tough bit. I am pretty much a data driven sort of person and to literally throw caution to the wind and just go with it was going against the grain and every instinct in my head.

My arms were hurting, as were my knees, inner thighs and my hands, trying to get my head to coordinate the graceful movement of the weight of a small horse was pushing it to the limit too especially the "trust" part of my brain which did not want to play at all.

The support from Libby and all the other ladies was amazing and at the end of the session, the round of applause was much appreciated. Before we headed home, I was offered the chance to try my hand at "hoop". Bloody hell, it took three or four people to get me off the ground and dangle, actually cling on for dear life let alone sit majestically in the hoop.

Ladies, one word - Respect!

The next morning, my body felt and looked like it had been beat up with bruises on my bruises and I ached in places I never knew I had places but what an experience.

Run #63 – Kirstie Leahy

I first met Kirstie back in February 2018 when she tried to muscle in on one of my 56notout runs with Karen Lines but her voice was already familiar. Kirstie is one of the bubbly presenters on TouchFM, one of our local radio stations and a great support of the challenge. Since February, Kirstie and I have met up a few times and I even managed to get her in the infamous ketchup outfit in the few days prior to the London marathon when Kirstie and the gang at the radio station promoted the many runners raising money for charity giving much appreciated encouragement at a pretty crucial time as the nerves kick in and excitement turns into panic. I love Kirstie's view of the world, even though as we chatted, life has had her ups and downs. I had a special route in mind today as I really wanted to leave my friendly DJ with a lasting memory. A route I have ran many times before and never fails to deliver.

Back in Kenilworth again with a chance to see the towns number one tourist attraction, the castle, from a different perspective. Heading away from town and into the countryside, the route I had chosen is great at keeping hidden the wow factor until the right moment to make an appearance. Swinging in a big loop with a combination of quite private access roads and well-trodden paths across arable fields, a glimpse of what lay ahead hinted between a gap in the trees. Kirstie was already enjoying the new route and stopped to take photos. I was pleased that the run was going well, shortly after, the main event came into view. The breath-taking unspoilt view of the ruins from the elevated crest of the path was the bonus.

I liked Kirstie's entry in my journal which pretty much confirmed what I have written :-

Dear Steve,

I first heard your lovely dulcet tones at the Leamington Parkrun, for once I was minding my own business struggling to get around after a particularly busy week. Somehow, we got chatting and our friendship grew from there. This is the part of my job which I truly enjoy, meeting people like you, making a difference, spreading love, positivity and hope across the world.

Thank you for a great run and hidden gems in Kenilworth, keep in touch.

And we have!

Run #64 – Rebecca Rogers and the Regency Runners

"Esse quam videri – be what you seem to be or be true to yourself."

A very different run and I had to just go with the flow. Having arranged to meet Rebecca Rogers, deputy head of my daughters' school, I realised anything could happen. Joining a regular evening session of the Regency Runners, for one night only I became an honorary member of the opposite sex as this group is a ladies only club. I like this group and have seen the blue tops becoming an increasingly familiar sight at local events. There are running clubs and running clubs, to quote their website: -

"Our philosophy at Regency Runners is to run for fun and fitness and we cater for ladies of all abilities from those who have just started running to those who are training for marathons. You can set your own goals and we'll support you along the way."

All about being the best you can, a familiar theme as it is also the motto of the Kingsley School, my daughters' school. Meeting Rebecca and the rest of the lovely ladies, I had no control and just did what I was told. It seemed that I needed no introduction as my arrival was not a surprise and the group new what I was about and before long, the talking was over, and I was in the thick of a training session. With the Jephson Gardens as the backdrop for speed circuits, the warm spring evening making the effort a pleasure. The alpha male did make a little appearance but soon retreated when I was clearly almost some great runners so settled to my comfort zone running with the slow yet determined runners which reading back in my journal, did not go unnoticed.

It was a delight to be an honorary lady and would put me in good shape for the next challenge when I would step, no leap, out of my comfort zone.

"Be you"

Of all the 365 days of the challenge, this is the day I will remember for the rest of my life. Emma, my stepdaughter and stalwart of social media throughout the year has a passion for the underdog.

Pride is very close to her heart and with many gay friends, Emma was keen that if we were going to do something at Pride, but it had to be done properly and didn't want it to attract the wrong attention. For me to dress up in drag could have so easily been misconstrued as taking the Mickey but it was not about that at all. I learnt so much about myself and those around me in those few hours. My blog the following day captures my mood and the day.

Our appearance in the parade took a lot of effort to bring it together, the design and printing of fliers along with the banner that would herald our arrival relied on the ever-supportive Sue Cox. The picket signs provided free of charge by the car industry legend "Ken the Chisel" and brought to life by Emma adding colour and impact to our contribution to the myriad of floats, walking groups and bands.

Throughout the last twelve months and beyond this crazy year, my family have never doubted me or my ideas. I consider my stepdaughters as my own and together with my own two, we are a family without question, but I am not your typical father figure and I appreciate that this cannot be easy sometimes. I always consider the impact I have on them, but I am in awe of the support they give me. My kids never doubt me, it's got to be tough to see your dad in a dress and make up. I know Julie did not care for it. The low point for her was helping me put on a bra (not mine for the record). "I shouldn't be doing this" she said, and she would not come anywhere near me all day.

It was only when we got home, and I returned to being myself did we become a couple again.

The blog ....

27th May 2018 - Being different

With only days remaining before the challenge year is over and the arrival of yet another candle on the birthday cake, I only have the last few challenges to complete and the end of an incredible year for the 56notout team.

Even when it looks like I am I having fun, all the challenges has a significant reason for being on the list. I have learnt so much about myself as I push myself physically, test my powers of persuasion, or come way out of my comfort zone, and sometimes a combination of them all. I plan to put pen to paper in the future and do into more detail as I open my heart to the world, but that is a later project.

The teams' involvement with Birmingham Pride was never on the original list, as were many of the challenges I have completed, it was a result of the kindness of Simon Baker from Birmingham Pride 2018, in response to a request for a market stall to do a little fundraising. Due to the Pride team's overwhelming requests for help, this was refused but Simon responded with the offer of a place in the parade through the streets of the second city and immediately the team went into overdrive and Ms 56notout was going to the ball! I had no choice but to embrace the challenge and just go with it, the arrival of sky-blue court shoes made my impending fate become real. Walking around the house in a pair of shorts and the shoes to "break them in" will be a lasting image for my family along with many others and I am sure counselling will be required at some point.

The day arrived and the transformation was complete, and I was ready to greet the world as Ms 56notout. I did not make a pretty woman and do not see myself on the cover of any magazines any time soon, but the team and I had the best day, the sun shone, the drinks flowed and we met so many lovely people who heard our story whether they wanted to or not!

Seeing people just being themselves was brilliant, no one judged, no one stared, and everyone could just be. The moto for 2018 "be you" was perfect and people just did that.

I felt underdressed to be honest and I was having a ball with the team, and no one gave a monkey's and I would love to go again.

Leaving the festival site and walking back to the railway station, my appearance, and being different became all too apparent. Blend in with the Saturday afternoon shoppers I did not.. and all of a sudden I became very vulnerable and not at all an ease with myself and the looks from passing strangers brought home to me what it was like to be outside of the circle and I so wanted to be in the safety of my own home and the chance to avoid the stares and comments. Not everyone was negative to me and I had the chance to chat with some lovely people from The USA on the station platform in Solihull and again had the chance to tell the story, they even kindly made an online donation.

An offhand, rather rude comment from the taxi driver hit home and I was very glad to be back in my own home, kick off my shoes and return to Steve.

An amazing day and a great team effort, a big thankyou to Simon Baker, festival co-ordinator Birmingham Pride 2018, it was a privilege to be part of this joyful event, and of course everyone who dressed up, waved a sign, carried a banner and walked and danced along with this 56 year old bloke in a sequinned frock as part of team 56notout on Saturday, Julie, Emma, Faye, Iain, Millie, Libby, Sam, Danni, Britanie, Zoe and Sam XXX

RUN #65 – TRISH GREEN

To have Trish as one of my 56notout runners was never in doubt, I liked running with new people for sure but to run with Trish was a must. We have ran together so many times along with numerous events and when we do, we start together and finish together with the miles in between full of fun and banter. We seem to bring the best out in each other, neither of us would be what you call athletes in the true sense of the word, but run we do. On race day the support from each other always gets us to the finish line and when one flags, the other lifts the spirit and the game continues. On a par with my eldest daughter Libby, I am not sure who has featured most in the event official event photographs, Coventry Half, the Two Castles, the Regency Run, the list goes on - which always featuring Trish with rosy red cheeks and a beaming smile accompanied with my good self-looking like a serial killer. Like many of us these days, work/life balance is a regular challenge for Trish and makes her running a little cyclic with the opportunity to put the trainers on often gazumped by a myriad of reasons. It was lovely to have a good catch up and the opportunity for some quality time to talk. I need Trish back running with me, I am sure we have a few more events left in us.....

Ride a unicycle

As long as I live, I am not sure I could ever ride a unicycle. I tried, I read the books, I watched the videos on YouTube, and I practised. I clung to the railings outside our home but as soon as I let go, I was heading for the floor. Reading the teach yourself book that Steve Shaw lent me did not help either and I quote *"most minor injuries to the upper inner thigh usually occurs when you attempt to grip the saddle as you fall..."* adding *"the genitals can also be injured when unicycling. Whereas females suffer less from such injuries, males risk crushing their testicles when over mounting the unicycle, or can be bruised when sitting on the saddle."*

It's all about balance, I do not have good balance. The challenge was to try to learn to ride a unicycle, I tried, oh how I tried -

honest! If the idea of the 60notout challenge ever sees the light of day then this is one idea that will be back on the list for 2021. By then the skin might have grown back on my shins. I will be sixty then and I will definitely need to get the luxury of soft crash mats. We best pencil in some training sessions Mr Shaw!

THEY THINK IT'S ALL OVER, IT IS NOW! CITY #10 – LICHFIELD

A fitting quote from the 1966 World Cup final and seemed to sum up the day and the year. The final day of the challenge year and as I turned 57, I wanted to end in style and with a bit of a flourish. Talk about last minute but it was just how it was, the intention was run the Bath Half Marathon but bad weather on race day resulted in the event being cancelled so I made Lichfield the destination for the tenth and final city. A beautiful place and not too far from work if you used your imagination, ok nowhere near the office but easier that doing two separate trips. Although early with the streets empty, the pavements looked like they were recovering from a very busy night.

I guessed that the city centre must have played host to some event the previous evening with litter, broken bottles and the occasional splatter of vomit spoiling what quaint and manicured little streets are, but only cosmetic with the clean-up process already underway.

I like Lichfield, a regular meeting place for old friends from up north and symbolic in a way as Lynn, was on my list to do something challenge related with but a bike accident put pay to our plans so was pleased that I could include her in my run if only in spirit. The magnificent three spired cathedral provided the iconic back drop to my last city run, #10 completing another challenge and with photographs taken along with the now routine video blog, I headed for work, a year on from when it all started but the day was far from over.

Run #66 – Nigel Harris

At the end of the workday, before travelling to the location for the final challenge, I manage to fit one last run in to make 66 in total. The last 10 had been bonus runs, with the run with 56 different people challenge being ticked off the list some weeks earlier but carried on just because I could. Runner 66 was a good one, as were the other 65 but to repeat of phrase I have used before, "every day's a school day", I learnt something new about my colleague and good friend Nigel Harris.

Nigel and I have always got on, working together for many years on the introduction of new processes and procedures, which is never easy involving meetings around Europe along with sometimes heated debates but regularly ending the day with a run and a beer or two.

As we ran, we talked about life and its meanings, religion and much more but strangely enough, very little of work. A stunning canal side route and a perfect last run setting me up nicely for the final challenge and the end of a life changing year.

TIME TO WALK THE WALK

The drive from the pub car park where I met Nigel to the venue for the final challenge was short and sweet, practically around the corner but long enough to ponder what lay ahead. I had fire walking on my list from that December night when the 56notout idea was born but proved to be very difficult to bring to fruition, cost and logistics being the main to prohibitors so for this challenge to happen, I would have to piggyback someone else event.

With time running out, a final plea on Facebook brought a positive result. Stephen Tabb, a friend of a friend came to my rescue. Steve was heavy involved in hockey and his club were holding a "Hockey for Heroes" fundraiser at including...... a fire walk and for a fee I could join them at their event.

I was concerned that it was risky leaving the final challenge until the very last day leaving no room for bad weather or something that was required the event being rescheduled (I did have something up my sleeve as a little insurance just in case but hopefully I would need it).

Arriving at the Old Silhillians Sports Club, I tracked down Steve and introduced myself and handed over the money before leaving him to concentrate on last minute arrangements for the rest of the fun filled evening, I grab a tasty burger from the BBQ and headed to watch a bit of hockey. I liked going to watch the ice hockey in Detroit back in the eighties but I had never taken a lot of notice of hockey played on grass however standing on touch line I really enjoyed being up close to the action and made the waiting fun and definitely helped settle the nerves.

As I watch the games, I could see the team from B.L.A.Z.E. setting up the fire walking area out of the corner of my eye and I was starting to feel anxious.

For the final challenge, I really wanted as many of my family with me as possible and to have a beer with them to celebrate my birthday too once the fire walk was over. It felt a long time since I left home early to drive to Lichfield, and I was looking forward to seeing Julie and the girls. Logistics were to be a feature of the final day and the family rallied around to make sure everyone was where they needed to be in time for the last challenge and with the help of our son in law, Iain together with Libby and her fiancée Tim, that's exactly what happened.

When the family arrived, the soon to be firewalkers had already been taken away in a room by the coach Karen Sterling from B.L.A.Z.E. to prepare us for the daunting task ahead.

Karen was a real character, larger than life and very Scottish, her preparation was brilliant and soon had us all feeling at ease. I didn't know what to expect, would I end up in A & E, would I BBQ my toes? Karen had an arsenal of techniques to call upon and within the hour we were all ready.

With the exception of Steve, who I had met an hour previous, I didn't know anyone else but once we had spent the time together, we felt like a family and everyone was pumped up and ready to go. The tension and power overwhelming, and when we walked out to walk the fire pit, the anticipation of what we were about to do was clear on our faces.

Soon it was time and "on mass" we left the room with Karen stood at the head of the corridor of embers. The spectators cheered and one by one we headed across the red-hot embers. Some it was my turn; I shouted my name and my declaration at the top of my voice, "I am Steve and I am ready" and with that I was fire walking.

My face said it all, one of the most empowering things I have ever done.

Reunited with my family and with a beer in hand, I celebrated the end of an amazing year.

3rd June 2017 - What we going to do now then.

We made it… 56 challenges completed or attempted in the case of the unicycle; we actually managed 58, not great at counting obviously!

Fire walking was a perfect end to an incredible year and although busy at times, and a little stressful, especially towards the end, when the 56notout idea was born on Friday 2 December 2016, I would never imagine that the year would have had such an impact on my life and those around me.

Many will know that I loved running with so many people over the last year and these people have made the year one that I will never forget. The support from family, friends, local companies and strangers who have become friends has brought me to tears many times, and I loved this quote written in my log book of runners from someone very close to me and it made me cry …..

"I may not have physically ran with you, but I have held your hand on roller coasters, swam through icy water, washed a million sets of running clothes, dressed you as woman, and watched as you knocked yourself out mentally and physically for something you believe in…… "

That's love that is….

Although the year is complete, you all know that this is not the end. 60notout has been mentioned, "You need a couple of years get planning Steve! ", was a comment made but let's see what the future brings.

The year started off with plan and a list like all good ideas should but some challenges never came to fruition whilst others that I always thought were a dead cert, somehow failed to get off the ground.

I never did get to breathe fire or shear a sheep, or introduce a band on stage, I came close, but no cigar, and as for a run with Daniel Craig – that didn't happen. I would still like to do these and if I ever get to meet Mr Bond, I'll let you know.

I will keep posting a blog from time to time to let you know what is going on, you just know that there will be something. I also plan to keep the just giving page open until the end of July, just in case. We might even top £5000, that would be amazing..

I thank you with all my heart and if you cannot find a nice person, be one.

The 31st May 2018 felt very different from the same day one year previous, looking back on an amazing year and wondered what I was going to do now. As I explained in the opening chapter of this book, we had a holiday planned and a little later, a party aptly titled "56 over and out" when we would get together with many of the people that had supported me, a chance to hand over the symbolic cheques to the charities and drink beer. The last time I had a beer in the Squirrel was Emma and Bolo's engagement party when I commenced probably the longest period without alcohol in my adult life so was good to return to celebrate the end of a great year.

NOT EVERY EGG'S A BIRD

People often ask me about the challenges that didn't make the final 56 or 58 as it actually turned out being adding a couple of bonus challenges along the way. I never dyed my hair blond, I really wanted to do this but this idea did not stand a chance of even making it to the maybe list. Other ideas like to make a guest appearance on a global podcast or appear in the pages of the national press which I thought would be stand a really good chance of seeing the finish line but alas not. Amazingly the chance to complete a challenge remotely connected with cars didn't make it either which is pretty surprising since I earn my living in the car industry.

My plan to swim from where I was born on the banks of the River Leam joining the River Avon and to our home in Warwick proved to be more than a little foolhardy even though I had been given the faint dime green light from the medical profession who were less worried about Weil's Disease and more about foreign objects beneath the water that I might be impaled on, so common sense prevailed and the challenge to swim in open water took another direction.

Busk, being a scarecrow, cheer leader, intro band, work on a building site, shear sheep and "walk the Wight" - the classic 26 miles walk across the beautiful Isle of Wight, were many of the challenges that didn't come off.

Another challenge that got away was appearing on TV, or did it? The team tried to get me on game shows, breakfast tv, you name it even Ant and Dec's Saturday night takeaway but without success. It was only when I chatted with Gary McKee in the latter weeks of the challenge year did I realise that I didn't really have a good track record, all my requests were based on "hopes and maybes" and as my 57th birthday grew ever nearer, I had the credibility but not on my side was time. I couldn't afford to pin my hopes on a maybe, I needed a firm offer of a television appearance before the end of May.

I posed a question earlier and to answer, yes, I did actually appear on TV, although I did not count it because I thought to count, I at least should say something and be named.

Emma, my eagle-eyed social media guru spotted me during the coverage of the London Marathon, in my tomato ketchup outfit in the crowd behind Radzi Chinyanganya, currently a presenter on the legendary children's show, Blue Peter as he interviewed preselected runners for the pre-race coverage. I must confess, I saw the filming going on but did know have a clue who he was. It was John Noakes, Peter Purvis and Valerie Singleton back in my day, pleased that this national institution has stood the test of time maybe because it has moved with the times whist keeping the DNA intact.

The team and I continued to bombard every TV show and exploited each and every potential opportunity to get my face on the telly but alas, so close but no cigar.

RIPPLES

I remember my run with Nicola Adams back in October and those words she wrote in my journal resonated in my head.

"Run with an open heart for today you will make ripples in the huge pond of life, tomorrow you will see what you have achieved."

We talked of ripples and the legacy of the challenge year, at the time I hadn't given a thought to the impact of the idea to be honest as I was focused on the moment, but now as I look back and look ahead, I can see what Nicola meant. The 56notout concept was never about raising money but more about raising awareness and although the year is over and I am another year older, the journey continues. As 2018 draws to an end and I am frantically getting my thoughts down for the book you have been reading, I am looking forward to the next chapter of my life including catching up with Kirstie Smith, reporter at the Leamington Courier and great supporter, always happy to find me some page space to tell the world of my latest exploits raising the profile of my charities, as she celebrates her own personal challenge year, Kirstie's 25 challenge for Bowel Cancer UK. I remember Kirstie asking me if I minded using the idea for her own personal journey. As she turned 25 on the 9th November 2017, her challenge year started. Half the age that her late father lost the fight to bowel cancer, she wanted to do something positive by doing something amazing for him. Kirstie's list was very different to mine, many with a 25 theme, but all with a meaning and not unlike my own, pushing her out of her comfort zone.

Another ripple came out of the blue from north of the border and took me by surprise. I have known Martin Lewis since the days of Rover Cars when a Mini actually was a Mini and not a Germanic reincarnation of the iconic creation of the late Sir Alec Issigonis, affordable to the masses instead of the price of a small house. I digress, Martin and I worked on some of the last few projects at the Longbridge plant. I worked in Engineering and Martin in Purchase and via social media have kept in touch. Martin had the sense to get out of the car industry heading to Scotland to work in banking "Huge congratulations on the achievements over the last year. I have been watching keenly and wondering if I can do the same. I am 50 this year so a few years to plan... but interested to know if anyone has taken up the baton from you?" You can guess the rest, we talked on the phone that night and the deal was done. My only request was that I wanted to do one of the challenges with him, still in the planning stage at the time this book goes to print but we have pencilled in seeing the sunrise from the top of Ben Nevis, now that will be special.

I will leave you with this :-

Every minute someone leaves this world behind.
We are all in "the line" without knowing it.
We never know how many people are before us.
We cannot move to the back of the line.
We cannot step out of the line.
We cannot avoid the line.

So, while we wait in line –

Make moments count.
Make priorities.
Make the time.
Make your gifts known.
Make a nobody feel like a somebody.
Make your voice heard.
Make the small things big.
Make someone smile.
Make the change.
Make love.
Make up.
Make peace.
Make sure to tell your people they are loved.
Make sure to have no regrets.
Make sure you are ready.

USEFUL CONTACTS :-

Follow "56notout" on Facebook
  www.facebook.com/56notout

Read the blog
  steveatherton.wordpress.com

Find out more about the amazing charities :-

Helping Hands
  www.helpinghandscharity.org.uk

Shelter
  www.shelter.org.uk

ACKNOWLEDGEMENTS

The 56notout year was one of the most amazing 365 days of my life but I could not have done it without the help and support of so many people.

Thank you to :-

Nigel Bonas for sowing the seed and Stuart Cock for providing the idea.

The amazing team at Helping Hands and Shelter for working so hard at the coal face supporting those who need help.

My wife Julie for always being with me, from the first shoots of the idea, to the last challenge, the highs, the lows and at times providing the voice of reason and for turning my blogs into English.

My family for getting behind this crazy idea 100%, family is everything. I am not the easiest of husbands, fathers, stepfathers or granddads.

My friends, old and new who donated, cheered, heckled, bought calendars, came to events and for just being there for me.

Local businesses who provided raffle prizes, supported events and continue to do so much for the homeless and rough sleepers in our towns and cities.

Team 56notout - Emma Pickering for making Social Media buzz, Susan Cox for all the help with everything arty.

Jane Bates, Matt Bartlett, Libby Atherton, Shelly Wilson and Peter Jones for making challenge number 57, the book, a reality.

David Chantrey for the cover picture taken during the London Marathon.

The local press and radio stations, Kirstie Smith from the Leamington Courier, Catherine Thompson at the Observer, Kirstie Leahy from TouchFM and all the team at BBC Coventry and Warwickshire.

To everyone to ran with me, challenged me, those who opened doors that were closed and made the impossible possible.

I thank all of you with all my heart.

And finally, to my mum and dad who never gave up on me and for making the person I am today.

Steve

Printed in Great
Britain
by Amazon

31267282R00181